THE SOCIETY OF SALTY SAINTS

"*They are holy people*
through whom the Kingdom of God is proclaimed daily
in their struggle to get by."

THE SOCIETY OF SALTY SAINTS

Story and Prayer ·from the Street

MICHEAL ELLIOTT

Illustrated by Glynda Massey

MEYER
STONE
BOOKS

Published in the United States by Meyer•Stone Books, a division of Meyer, Stone, and Company, Inc., 714 South Humphrey, Oak Park, IL 60304

Cover design: Terry Dugan Design

Manufactured in the United States of America
91 90 89 88   5 4 3 2

Meyer•Stone ISBN 0-940989-14-X

To my wife,
Janice Garner Elliott,
the smartest person I know

Contents

Introduction

Someone coined a new phrase: "inner-city churches." That was not long ago. Actually it is a euphemism. It is a nice name for that which has been abandoned, moved away from, given up on. When the fashionable lived in mansions in the cities the places where they gathered on Sunday mornings were called the great churches of the land. Even *The Church*. Now churches, even *The Church*, are located in the suburbs.

One by one we watched them go, leaving behind massive steeples and structures. And leaving people. Little people we are prone to think. Drunks, bums, addicts, whores, the poor, streetpeople? No! Just people. People we pin those appellations upon to distinguish them from real people. Sometimes we quote, "Inasmuch as ye have done it unto the least of these..." and do nice things for them. Especially on religious and nationalistic holidays. It is further deprivation. For who says they are the *least?* Perhaps they are the greatest and we are the least.

Whatever, whether greatest or least, there are those who have chosen to "be with them." And is not that the litmus test of faithfulness? *The Society of Salty Saints* is a portrait of some who have made that choice. Jesus didn't really ask us to do very much. He talked about such things as a cup of cold water. Sometimes what we call the *great* churches get caught up in trying to design a global sprinkler system so that everyone will have a drink. Meanwhile, those near at hand, the ones in the ditch, go unrefreshed. Within these pages we see service to those near at hand. We see celebration and lamentation, joy and sorrow. We meet people, real people. People like a one-eyed, near deaf woman who would never be "ordained" by the steeples because she is old, or because she is a *she,* or has no theological training, or perhaps a dozen other reasons. But as we walk with her we know that God's hands have been laid upon her.

We see Buena, a bald, elderly woman, chewing tobacco (yes, in church) who is a saint. And Grace, named well. Mary, Charlene, and dozens of others. (Strange that so many of the "inner-city church" are women.) But there are men too. Men like Bruce, an alcoholic who gave up his last bit of wine for communion. And a church roach who got the life stomped out of him so that the service might continue.

An introduction should be just that. I resent it when someone introduces me to Mr. Jones and then tells me everything there is to be known about him, trying to establish a relationship that won't be because it is rushed. Just tell each of us the name of the other. We'll take it from there.

So, Brothers and Sisters, meet the Society of Salty Saints. If I hadn't thought you would hit it off I wouldn't have brought you together.

WILL D. CAMPBELL

Acknowledgments

The members the Jefferson Street Baptist Chapel in Louisville, Kentucky, are the down and out, the homeless, the young, the old, and the poverty-stricken of Louisville's inner city. More than that, however, they are saints. They are holy people through whom the Kingdom of God is proclaimed daily in their struggle to get by.

Each of the stories recounted here is true. That is important because each has to do with the real faith of real people. Many believe that Christian community in the inner city is impossible. The "salty saints" of the Jefferson Street Baptist Chapel, however, are just such a community, one that gives us glimpses of faith. The greatest theological truths grow out of the struggles that make up everyday lives.

I am thankful to the people from whose lives these stories are drawn. The commitment of their coming together is a testimony to the power of the living God in the world today. These brothers and sisters help blind eyes to see.

There are some individuals who merit special attention, although I could never mention them all. Dr. Russell Bennett, my friend and supervisor, allowed me to take time off to begin writing. To Rev. Cindy Weber, Janice Money, and Melessia Stillwell, my colleagues in the ministry who carried more than their share of my load while I wrote, I respond with too shallow thanks and very much love. Father Vernon Robertson continues to point out to me how great it is to be a Southern Baptist. My parents, Billy and Margaret Elliott, housed me and fed me while I wrote. My brother, David, and my sister, Angie, are constant sources of encouragement. My in-laws, Carl and Sarah Garner, help me to take a real vacation every year. Carol Grizzard proofread the manuscript for me and deserves a medal. Bill Thomason forged it into a real book.

Claude Drouet, Bill and Kathy Berry, and Guy and Anita Sayles continue to be the best friends a person could ask for. Larry Desolier is a constant source of love and affirmation. Special thanks to Kelly Elpee for discussions on the banks of the Ohio. My grandparents, Rev. Ira and Edith Carver, showed me what it is to be a follower of Jesus in the first place.

More than anyone else, however, Janice, Jeremy, and Kristen put up with me while I wrote. It is to them that I offer the most thanks. While I saw love in the inner city, these three help me to explore its depths.

THE SOCIETY OF SALTY SAINTS

"Glimpses of the Kingdom
do indeed occur every day in the Society of Salty Saints.
Very often, despite evidence to the contrary,
the Holy Spirit is on the move...."

Inner-City Churches

Inner-city churches are a testimony to the endurance of the church in modern-day America. They are located in neighborhoods that need what churches have to offer, but lack the resources to maintain the congregations. Indeed, many of the congregants of inner-city churches no longer live in the neighborhood at all; they moved out at the first opportunity. Many find new churches closer to their new homes, but a surprisingly large number maintain their commitment to the old Christian family.

These churches struggle to keep their identity alive. The community they serve is typically poor and overwhelmed with the problems that poverty brings. Alcoholism and drug addiction prevail. Youth roam the neighborhood unattended. Housing is in disrepair and, these days, disappearing. Unemployment is commonplace. Violence is the currency of many relationships, and loneliness is the sad companion of too many lives. The homeless, the hungry, and the proud all need the services of the church. It is to them that the inner-city church proclaims "good news to the poor, healing to the sick, deliverance to the prisoner, recovery of sight to the blind, freedom to the oppressed, and the acceptable year of the Lord."

With very few resources and great liabilities, many inner-city churches keep struggling forward. Their ministries center around preaching and social services. They maintain clothing closets and food pantries. Children's ministries are provided; inner-city children will show up for just about anything. Congregations are a mixed lot of hangers-on, poor children, senior adults, single middle-aged folk, alcoholics, and other would-be worshippers. In other circumstances these people would never be found together. Yet in the name of Jesus they are an obstinate light for the neighborhood and an alternative life for the lost and oppressed.

Success for inner-city churches is not easily measured. They cannot boast of numbers the way that many of the "stronger" congregations do. Downtown churches typically have a small number of worshippers. While the fields are white for harvest, the workers are few.

Nor can downtown churches point to their buildings the way that many suburban congregations can. The edifice of the inner-city congregations is usually old, run down, in disrepair, and, especially when it comes to questions of heating and cooling, viewed as a liability.

Neither can inner-city churches point to their pastors as testimony to their success. Most ministers would never consider the inner-city as a viable area in which to carry out their calling. Only a few willingly go to the inner city. Most seek churches with more workers and better buildings. Most, too, seek churches that compensate with an appropriate salary package; inner-city churches can barely manage the electric bill. People who wind up as inner-city ministers are usually the semi-retired, part-timers, students, or radicals who cannot fit in elsewhere.

What, then, is success to an inner-city congregation? Perhaps the endurance of the people is an appropriate measurement. Inner-city congregations are slow to give up and allow the church to die. They are called too old and set in their ways to revive their ministries and make them "successful" according to other measurements. And yet, they continue to maintain their existence against all odds. They still hope against all hope that the Spirit will move, resurrection will occur, and inner-city neighborhoods will be transformed into Christian communities.

Glimpses of the Kingdom do indeed occur every day in the society of salty saints. Very often, despite evidence to the contrary, the Holy Spirit is on the move, resurrections are occurring, and a Christian community, albeit very different from the one in the suburbs, is developing. Inner-city churches still wish to save the world like their suburban counterparts. But they have learned a lesson that the Talmud teaches and Jesus exemplified: the world can only be saved one neighbor at a time.

While downtown churches appear dead on the outside, there is a spirit within waiting to be acknowledged. When individuals cry out in faith for healing, deliverance, fellowship, or freedom from bondage, the Spirit moves. The Spirit hears these cries of faith. If the believer is watching, he or she may very well catch a glimpse of the Kingdom on earth as it is in heaven.

The Kingdom observed here does not shake mountains or topple governments, although it has paved the way for such changes on occasion. Likewise, only rarely does the Kingdom express itself in terms of drastic changes in public policies or in the presence of political leaders. As Robert McAfee Brown has stated: "No Savior will ever sleep in the White House." Most often, the Kingdom does not draw that much attention to its presence. Rather, the presence of the Kingdom is quiet, unassuming, and consistent.

Inner-city churches maintain the example that Simeon set in the birth narratives of Jesus. They continue to wait. They may be old and crumbling and set in their ways, but they refuse to be daunted by all the evidence that salvation may not be coming. Like the old man who patiently waited on the birth of Jesus, inner-city churches refuse to die. They hang on for just one glimpse of the coming Kingdom (see Luke 2:25–35).

"The witness of their faith is great,
for they offer something that the rest of today's urban society is losing —
constancy in commitment to the church."

Part I

MATRIARCHS OF THE STREET

ONE OF THE FIRST THINGS that strikes a visitor to an inner-city congregation is the disproportionate number of women in the church. Most often, they are very old and very faithful. Refusing to leave the fellowship that gave them so much, they struggle for ways to keep the flame alive in bleak circumstances. They often can do little more than show up whenever the church doors are open. And show up they do.

One is reminded of the prophetess Anna (Luke 2:36ff). A very old woman who had lived most of her life as a widow, she "never left the Temple but worshiped day and night, fasting and praying." I suspect that she never left the Temple because she never had to. It was always open. It took care of all her needs.

Although inner-city churches are usually open only on Sundays and, perhaps, for a mid-week prayer service, the spirit of Anna

lives on in countless senior citizens. There are widows every bit as
faithful as the old prophetess. The witness of their faith is great,
for they offer something that the rest of today's urban society is
losing — constancy in commitment to the church.

1

The Hardness of Belief

Mrs. Flood is an old, one-eyed crippled woman who has lived in the inner city since before there was such a term. She wears one dark lens in her glasses which, combined with her wavy white hair, gives the impression that she bore pirates for children. The knee brace on her right leg and her thick wooden cane accompany her slow pace. She doesn't walk so much as shuffle her feet. Ever so slowly she makes her way down the street to attend church. She never misses a service unless she is bed-ridden. Mrs. Flood is so deaf that she cannot hear much that goes on during the worship service, but she is unfailing in her attendance.

Fanni Flood is, after all, a Christian. More than anything else, she is a believer, and there are few who believe harder. When times are good she believes that God is saying, "Job well done." When times are bad she claims, "Honey, you just believe and everything will be all right."

Even when her first husband beat her and the baby so much that Mrs. Flood's body bled and the baby died, she still believed that Jesus was present somehow. "As he was hitting me and as the baby was crying and as he was cussing, I saw Jesus."

"What did he look like?"

"Honey," says this eighty-eight-year-old, completely undaunted by the question, "he was a light. And he came to me and he said, 'Don't you worry now. I am here.'"

Mrs. Flood really believes it. More than that, she practices what she believes. Her small apartment in the senior citizen's highrise has been an overnight shelter for the city's homeless, a

fellowship center for the mentally ill, and the sight of a common
table for strangers who are hungry.

"Mrs. Flood, you simply cannot go around having strangers in
your home."

"I believe the Bible says that I am supposed to have strangers
in my home."

"But Mrs. Flood, it might be dangerous."

"I believe that I'm not supposed to worry about things like
that. God says that he will protect his own."

"But Mrs. Flood, someone might try to hurt you."

"Honey, did I ever tell you about the time Jesus came to me
when I was being beaten?..."

I believe that she believes.

●

*...[and the father said] "And if you can do anything, take
pity on us and help us."*

*"If you can?" said Jesus. "Everything is possible to those
who believe."*

*Immediately the boy's father exclaimed, "I do believe; help
me overcome my unbelief!"*

[Mark 9:14ff]

●

Lord,
You said, "Everything is possible to those who believe."
That's hard for me to believe.
Most times it strikes me as absurd. The world demands that I
    believe only what I can see, touch, taste, feel....
Some people, like Fanni Flood, don't seem to have my problem.
    Instead of hard belief, they have a belief that is hard, belief
    that has stood up to the worst the world could do to them.
They believe you are always with them.
    They seem to know something I do not.
    You say believe.
When I pray, Lord, I wonder if you hear.
You never answer the way that I want you to.
My knees crack out a response.
My mind looks for answers.
Mostly, there is silence.
"Jesus? Are you there?"
Belief is hard for me.
But I believe that I want to believe.
Lord, help my unbelief.

                                                              Amen.

2

The Ordeal of Commitment

Mary grimaced with pain as she climbed the stairs leading up to the chapel. With one hand she tightly held the bannister. With the other, she used her cane to shove all her weight from one step to the next. Sweat began to pour down her face on only the third step. There were seven more to go. When someone ran down to offer assistance, she quickly exclaimed, "I've had years of practice doing this all by myself, thank you!"

Then she stopped and rested. Balancing herself on the third step she said to no one in particular, "I wonder when they're going to get that chair-lift that the preacher keeps talking about. I sure could use it." Then with determination on her face, she began the ordeal of her commitment again.

For forty years her commitment had been unfailing. She had held virtually every position in the church. Always waiting to see if anyone else would take the job, she would say yes when no one else would. Currently, she was the librarian, the Sunday School superintendent, and the church clerk. The only time she missed a service was when she fell and broke her hip again.

She hated to miss church. "It's my family," she would say. "When my son took an overdose of drugs, the church was there for me. When I have to go to the hospital, people from the church take me. When I am alone, they come to see me. I'm not the one who is committed. They are."

"Who are they? The people in the church change so much," a young student from the seminary once asked her.

"It doesn't matter. The church is the church. The church is

12

people. But the church is more than just the people. It's ... it's ... I don't know. But when I'm there I know that it's something special. I know that I'm better off for it."

As people darted up the stairs past her, she paused and greeted each one. "Good morning. Isn't it good to be here?" Watching her desire to come, I knew that it was good.

•

And he said to her, "Daughter, your faith has made you well; go in peace."

[Luke 8:41–48]

•

Lord,
the faith I have is dwarfed by others.
Others believe in ways that I do not understand.
Their commitment is unfailing.
    Their consistency is full of integrity.
        Their faith is complete.
My faith is shallow and simple.
I demand reason from you and safe distance from others.
My commitment is first to my own comfort, ...
    both spiritual and physical.
Let me have faith like this woman's.
Let the ordeal of my commitment be the crown of your glory.
                        Amen.

3

The Prize Fight

Buena was a big woman. She weighed every bit of 250 pounds. Whenever she entered a room, everyone knew it. From the backwoods of rural Kentucky, Buena had a high nasal country twang. "Now I'mma gonna teel ya sometin," she would say. Yet it was not only her voice or her size that commanded attention.

For one thing, she was absolutely bald. This is not to say that she went around with her head uncovered. She knew of all the biblical references regarding women and covered heads, and she usually wore a wig. Wigs, however, sometimes turn upon one's head, especially if that head is totally bald. Often she would enter a room with her wig slightly askew, with part coming down over one ear and one side high above the other. People tried not to notice. It was hard.

Whenever she did not wear a wig, Buena would wear a bandana wrapped around her head — usually only on the hottest days of summer. She looked like a white Aunt Jemima, except for the scar that ran across her face. She never mentioned how she got it.

Buena always carried an empty Maxwell House coffee can with her, which served as her portable spittoon. During church services, Buena was the "Amen corner," and there was no need to have more than one person in it. Whenever she saw that the preacher was "caught up in the spirit," she would spit into her can and shout Amen. "The-Whitt, Po-WEE — AMANN!"

If a minister asked her about tobacco in church, Buena responded, "Now preacher, I'a don't put words inta yer mouth, so don't teel me what ta put in mine."

"But during church?"

"Helps me ta hear," she would reply.

For years, Buena ran the clothing closet. During the clothes closet sale, she sat by the door, stomach between her legs, Maxwell House coffee can in one hand, and the other sitting on top of the cash box. She would bellow out to the waiting customers: "Now ya'll listen. There be good stuff in here, so no runnin', no fightin', and no stealin'!" After she gave the signal, everyone would rush in and begin rummaging through the racks of clothes. Buena sat by the door and watched.

On one occasion there were many new clothes and the crowd was huge. Elderly women have a difficult time going through the racks when the crowds are so large. Rather than fight the crowd for the best selections, they often stay off to one side, looking through the piles of shoes, belts, and old toys.

Today there was a prize to be found in the piles — a pair of quality work boots. Buena had hidden the boots so that there would not be a mad dash for the shoe pile. Two elderly women began to rummage through the pile. At the same moment, both discovered a boot. Their eyes glowed. Here was something, not for their husbands or sons — both probably long gone — but for themselves! Boots would keep their feet warm in the drafty, impossible-to-heat houses that they lived in. Boots would help them to get around in the snow. Boots were more dependable than children and certainly more valuable than the fifty cents Buena had marked on the price tag.

Each woman grabbed a boot at the same moment. Each felt a tug. With horror both realized that the other had hold of one of the boots. Buena had tied their strings together.

"They're mine! I saw them first!"

"No you didn't! I did!"

"Let go!"

A tug-of-war broke out. The other shoppers paused and saw with envy what the two were fighting over. The only sounds in the room were the grunts and groans of the two women fighting for their prized possession.

Buena observed the scene with minimal concern. Indeed, she appeared amused. After allowing the tug-of-war to go on for a few minutes, she spat, "The-Whitt! Po-WEE!" Heaving her great stomach up between her legs she slowly made her way over to the prize fight. With quick action she jerked a butcher knife out from her apron and, in one motion, cut the string that tied the boots together.

"Thar," she calmly said, "now ya both got one. I don't wanna heer nother peep outa ya."

Buena sat down. The shoppers resumed their shopping. And each lady bought a boot.

•

...And the King said, "Divide the living child in two, and give half to the one and half to the other."

[1 Kings 3:25]

•

Lord,

I try to do the right thing.

If people do me wrong, I may get mad, but I try to work things out with them.

I try to forgive. I try to forget.

I try to do things for others.

I give old clothes to the poor, some money to the church and to charities, and sometimes, I give my time to good work.

But time is money, Lord.

Time is to be spent with my family.

Time is to be spent with me.

The church would take all of my time if I let it. There are others to do your work. I try to do my part.

The needs are so many. I couldn't possibly make that much of a difference.

Life is a difficult maze of questions with too few answers, Lord. I try to choose correctly. The pressures are so great for me to do things this way and not that.

Give me wisdom, Lord,

so that I will struggle with the right questions and not waste my time on the wrong ones.

Give me courage,

so that I will not be afraid of the questions or the answers or of where they might lead me.

Give me faith,

so that I will be able to enter into the middle of difficult situations and will know what to do.

Give me peace, Lord,

so that I will be able to live with the choices that I make.

                                                              Amen.

4

The Evidence of Faith

It was a special Sunday night service. The faithful few who came to church in the evenings — no more than eight or ten — came to remember the Lord's Supper. The church building was dark, lit only by candle light. The only music was led by the seminary student who had come to play his guitar. "Let us break bread together on our knees," they sang.

The minister asked if there were special concerns that anyone would like to share. "Remember my sister, Illa," asked one. "She is in the hospital again."

"Pray that I'll find a job," said another, as he made his weekly request.

The seminary student who had played the guitar cleared his throat. "My wife and I have just discovered that we are going to have another child." Everyone grinned. A few people laughed out loud. The young man smiled and continued. "Anyway, we have been here for about a month. We've run through all the money that we have saved. I haven't been able to find a job yet. This week has been particularly bad. Pray that we will be able to get through it."

Everyone prayed. Then the plate with the bread was passed around. When it came to old Mr. Berry he mistook it for the offering plate and stood up taking a few coins out of his pocket, dropped them into the tin plate, and passed it on.

The following Sunday morning after Sunday School the student was walking with his wife and little boy down the hall toward the sanctuary. Looking up, he saw that their way was blocked. Buena stood with four or five others huddled behind her. Maxwell House coffee can in hand, she said, "We be got something for ya." The other ladies smiled, but said nothing. Buena thrust her hand forward and placed an envelope in his hand. The bewildered student looked down and found that it was full of money.

"We just want ya ta know that we love ya and like the way that ya play the guitar." The stunned student could not believe his eyes. Here were poor senior citizens, all of them widows on fixed incomes, giving to someone they barely knew. He knew that fixed incomes do not go as far in the inner city as they do in other places. He knew that these ladies really did not have it to give. Yet, here they were, giving anyway.

"I can't take this," he protested.

Buena spit. It was not her usual hard, fast The-Witt, Po-WEE! This was a long, slow drip of brown juice into the can. "Look'ee hare," she said. "We be knowing what it's like to be without. This is far ya." The silent, smiling ladies said nothing. They just nodded their heads.

Tears began to build up in the student's eyes. He had always been on the giving end when it came to help. His middle-class background never prepared him to be graceful when it came to receiving. His pride kept making him say that he could not take their money. He knew that they were poor.

The ladies would not listen to his protest. Finally, he stuck the money into his pocket. He hugged each of the ladies. His wife cried. His little boy stared at the whole scene in respectful awe. Then they entered the sanctuary and worshipped.

•

And all who believed were together and had all things in common; and they sold their possessions and goods and distributed them to all, as any had need. And day by day, attending the Temple together and breaking bread in their homes, they partook of food with glad and generous hearts, praising God and having favor with all of the people. And the Lord added to their number day by day those who were being saved.

[Acts 2:44–47]

He looked up and saw the rich putting their gift into the trea-sury; and he saw a poor widow put in two copper coins. And he said, "Truly, I tell you, this poor widow put in more than all of them; for they gave out of their abundance, but she out of her poverty put in all the living that she had.

[Luke 21:1–4]

•

Lord,

it is more blessed to give than it is to receive, but I do not seem to be able to do either one very well.

When it comes to what I give I am embarrassed.

People who have much less than I give much more than I do. I give out of my abundance. I have seen others who give out of their poverty. I am ashamed of the comparison between their contribution to your Kingdom and mine.

Forgive me, Lord, for the arrogance of my tithe.

When it comes to receiving from others, I am also ashamed. Some receive gifts gracefully. I do not. And Lord, how can I receive your gift of grace when I cannot even gracefully receive what others offer me?

Forgive me, Lord, of the pride that dictates so much of the way that I live my faith.

When it comes to my time, keep me from writing a check so that I will not have to spend any of myself.

When it comes to my money, keep me from sharing with only token amounts so that I can hoard most for myself.

When it comes to my needs, help me to share them as I do my strengths, so that as I come to know others, others will come to know me.

Remind me, Lord, that the evidence of your resurrection is a living and giving fellowship.

Give me the courage and the will to leave the comforts of my individualism for participation in the fellowship of believers.

Amen.

5

A Thankless Job

She lives a quiet life. A widow for many years, she took care of her mother until her mother died. Then she took care of her dog until the dog died. Now she lives alone taking care of herself. Occasionally, family will come to visit for a few days or someone from the church will drop by. Most of the time, however, she is alone with her house.

Grace does get around better than most senior citizens I know. I often see her walking to the store or waiting for the bus. She attends programs for her age group all over the city. She likes to go shopping. She volunteers at her church.

Almost every Monday is spent with Mabel sorting through bags of donated clothes. Each week there is a mountain of clothes to be sorted, sized, and folded, and each week Grace is there. It is a thankless job; she never sees the results of her work, which provides countless people with clothing. Each morning ten to fifteen homeless men and women work through the sorted clothes and find something to wear. Senior citizens purchase clothes each week from the church's clothes sale for seniors. Neighborhood mothers rummage through the clothes every Tuesday and find items for themselves, their children, and their friends. Many a passerthrough has discovered a coat to wear on a cold winter's day.

But all that Grace and Mabel see are the mountains of unsorted clothes that greet them every Monday morning. Often discouraged, but never defeated, they slowly begin their thankless job. Week after week. Year after year. The job of clothing the naked.

•

Then the righteous will answer him, "Lord, when did we see
you hungry and feed you, or thirsty and give you something to
drink? And when did we see you as a stranger and welcome
you, or naked and clothe you?..." And the King will answer
them, "Truly, I say to you, as you did it to one of the least
of these my brothers and sisters, you did it to me...."

[Matthew 25:37–40]

•

Lord,
I feel called,
    but not to a thankless task.
I need affirmation,
    encouragement,
        uplifting,
           support.
I need praise;
    public praise...
        private praise...
           ceaseless praise.
It is not for the praise of others that we are to work.
When we boast, we are to boast of you,
    not ourselves.
Our reward is not in the words of people but in other things.
Our reward is when the hungry are fed,
    the lonely are visited,
        the thirsty quenched,
           the stranger welcomed,
               the naked clothed....
Too often I do not do these things to satisfy you, Lord, but to
    receive the praise and the thanks of those I do it for.
That is the wrong reason.
Remind me that thankless tasks are often your task.
Help me to be satisfied with that.
Help me to control my ego.
Help me to make my desires the same as yours.
Thy will be done on earth,
    and in my life,
        as it is in heaven.

Amen.

6

The Advent of Christ

On a hot August day Buena finally went to the doctor. There she discovered that the great stomach that she carried around was not stomach at all. It was cancer. "We're sorry," said the doctor, "but it appears that because the cancer has progressed to the point that it has, surgery is out of the question. There will be some medication that will help in the short term, but there is little that can be done, medically, over the long haul."

"What ya be sayin'?" she asked.

The doctor cleared his throat. "You have about six weeks to live."

Buena lifted the Maxwell House coffee can toward her mouth. The-Witt, Po-WEE! She spit into the can and the sound echoed down clean, antiseptic smelling halls. "We'll see," she said.

As with almost everything else, Buena proved whatever people said about her to be wrong. A few weeks after seeing the doctor that day, she became bed-ridden, but she lived well into the month of March — one last act of defiance against the doctors.

When people visited her, they would often find her in good humor with Bible and Maxwell House coffee can nearby her bed. Sometimes the visitor would have to wait until she could get her wig on. She loved to be visited, and always asked about the church. She would often ask the visitor to act as a carrier for her. Then making sure that none of her family was watching, she would open the desk by the bed and take out two twenty dollar bills. "This be my offerin'. Be sure ta tell the preacher, tat I'mma tithing my Bingo winnings." Buena loved Bingo.

"Buena," the preacher would sometimes say, "You're not supposed to play Bingo. It's gambling."

"Naw," she would reply, "it's all right. So long as ya remember to tithe your winnings."

When the Christmas season descended upon the church, the congregation gathered for their celebration of the birth of the baby Jesus. The congregation had sponsored a toy sale, two hundred Christmas baskets for the hungry, and a special holiday meal for the homeless. Now it was time for them to celebrate.

After a pot luck meal, the church family gathered around the piano and began to sing Christmas carols. There were homeless men singing next to students and elderly women. Whites stood with their arms around blacks. Wealthy people hugged the poor. The dividing walls of hostility had crumbled on this special day.

After much singing, Claude suggested that we walk over to Buena's house and sing her some Christmas carols. Everyone thought this an excellent suggestion, so the entire church marched down the block and around the corner to where she lived. We knocked and waited for Buena to put her wig on. Then we were allowed in.

The group of twenty or so crowded around the bed. Buena was obviously pleased that so many had come. She tried, of course, not to show it. We sang a few songs and Buena sang along. Claude asked, "Buena, what is your favorite? Let us sing it for you."

With no hesitation she responded, "Silent Night."

We began to sing. "Silent Night, Holy Night . . . " And it was. It was a clear, cold evening with a star-filled sky. We all felt good about how we were spending it.

Suddenly, however, with the church family gathered around Buena's bed, tears began to roll down her face. Then tears began to stream down the faces of every visitor. Our church, which many considered a dying church, was singing carols to a dying lady. The carol took on new meaning as the tiny congregation sang to Buena. "Sleep in heavenly peace, . . . sleep in heavenly peace. . . . "

The fellowship of believers filed out of her bedroom one by one. Some hugged her good-bye. Others kissed her tobacco-stained mouth. Down the frozen sidewalks that led back to the building that is called the church, no one said a word.

●

There is one body and one Spirit — just as you were called to one hope when you were called — one Lord, one faith, one baptism; one God of all, who is over all and through all and in all.

[Ephesians 4:5–6]

•

Lord,
sometimes our lives are filled with the bright lights of a happy
season, the gay music of a joyous heart, and the glowing
warmth of good friends and good times.
Sometimes we hear the choirs singing and the children laughing
and the people rushing about in an effort to give gifts to
others.
Yet, O Lord, sometimes we see beyond the bright lights and the
gay music. Sometimes we see other things:
The faces of parents who are worried for their children.
The elderly waiting alone in desperate hopes that there will be
more than a token visit from people who are too busy to love.
Men and women attempting to numb the pain of life by pouring
alcohol or injecting drugs into their bodies.
The dull-eyed,
    the empty faced,
        the broken hearted,
            the haters of life,
                the walking dead.
O, Lord, give me compassion so that I will pray for those who
have nothing and those who feel nothing, so that they, and I,
will be moved to action.
Give me the power to give without attaching strings to the gifts
that I so often want to place upon them.
Give me the desire to share the knowledge of what the Christ is
all about.
Most of all, give me the love of the Christ, so that I can give it to
others, so that the Lord will not flee from my life.

Amen.

"Refusing to leave the fellowship that gave them so much,
they struggle to keep the flame alive in bleak circumstances."

THE UPSIDE-DOWN KINGDOM
Luke 4:16–30

He opened the book and found the place where it is written: "The Spirit of the Lord is upon me to preach good news to the poor. He has sent me to proclaim release to the captives and recovery of sight to the blind, and to set at liberty those who are oppressed, to proclaim the acceptable year of the Lord." And he closed the book and gave it back to the attendant, and sat down; and the eyes of all who were in the Synagogue were fixed upon him. And he began to say to them, "Today this Scripture has been fulfilled in your hearing."

And when the men came to him, they said, "John the Baptizer has sent us to you, saying, Are you the one who is to come or shall we look for another?..." And he answered them, saying, "Go and tell John what you have seen and what you have heard: the blind receive their sight, the lame walk, lepers are cleansed, the deaf hear, the dead are raised up, the poor have good news preached to them. Blessed are those who take no offense at me."

Good news to the poor has to mean taking away whatever makes them poor (and therefore different, unaccepted, scorned). They would no longer be poor. They would be accepted, secure, and satisfied. Release to the captive means freedom — no more jail! Blind people seeing, lame people running, deaf people hearing.... The Acceptable Year of the Lord — the Kingdom of God — is what Jesus called it.

Many of us are afflicted in other ways as well. It is not just iron bars that hold folks in, but bottles, careers, and a host of forces that we cannot escape. Many are blind to what they do not wish

27

to see. Many refuse to hear words that are spoken for their own benefit. Some are sick with fear that their uncontrollable lives are taking them where they do not wish to go. A few are dead. They may not be physically dead, but there is more than one way not to live. We can be dead when we are alone; we can be dead when we are excluded by others; the worse kind of death, though, is when we are not at peace with ourselves.

The question that John the Baptizer asked is also our question: "Jesus, are you the one who is to come or shall we look for another?" The ones who ask this today are imprisoned — whether by physical bars or psychological ones. They are poor in spirit, or poor in health. They are those who are oppressed — by people, by bottles, or by dead-end lives. Some ask louder than others. Some are weary of asking. Some give up the search for the answer.

It is not the words that provide the answer, of course. We hear those all of the time. "Jesus is the answer!" "Give your heart to him and everything will be all right." "Jesus will put your life back in order." Most of us desperately want to believe these words. But too many people have never gotten their lives back together again, even though they said all the right words. We quit hearing the words of Jesus because they do not seem to work for us. Refusing to pretend that they do, we place no more stock in the "old-time religion." We become deaf and blind and dead to the word of Jesus.

So where is the good news? Where are the lives that are being put back together? Where is the release from captivity that binds our faith? Why can't we free ourselves from the things that we do not really want to do any more? Why do so many fall down after trying to put some order in their lives... again? What is this good news?

When John's disciples asked *our* question — "Are you the one who is to come or should we look for another?" — Jesus answered them. He did not reply with cheap talk and empty promises, but with deeds: "Go and tell John what you have seen and what you have heard: the blind receive sight, the lame walk, lepers are cleansed, the deaf hear, the dead are raised up, and the good news is preached to the poor." The good news begins with the fact that Jesus answered.

When Jesus answered, he was saying, yes, he is the one. The Kingdom starts with Christ. "With the birth of the Savior Son," writes C. S. Song in *Proclaiming the Acceptable Year,* "God intensified his revolution within the world. And what a revolution! It strives to liberate the poor from their poverty and the rich from their riches. It struggles to liberate the powerless from their powerlessness and the powerful from their power. It is a revolution that liberates truth from lies that corrupt human hearts and pollute human community." With Jesus the good news is that the world we are now living in is on its way out. The new Kingdom of God is underway.

God's Kingdom is not the same as the old way. God's Kingdom is based on God's way of doing things, not ours. God's way inverts the ways of human beings. The proclamation of good news to the poor, healing for the sick, release to the captive, all sound so positive and reasonable that the shocking inversion may not be visible to many. Things will be turned upside down when God reigns in the lives of people and in the world.

But, many will say, the bills are still mounting on the kitchen table. Captivity still keeps too many from freedom. So many are blind to the things that they want to see, but cannot. Too many are deaf to the options available to them. Countless folk end up feeling that the spirit of Jesus may be close by, but they need more than abstract spirits.

We do not have to live up to the expectations of the old world. We never could anyway. The old world expects us to get ahead at any and all cost. It expects us to be successful at whatever we do. It expects us to look like winners, to feel like winners, and to *be* winners. The old world does not have any space for those who have tried and failed. It has no space for individuals who have never recovered from past mistakes. The old world is not concerned with those who continue to fail in life regardless of how hard they try.

The good news of Jesus is that there is a choice. There is an option. We can choose to be a part of a new, different way. We can be a part of a new Kingdom where Jesus inverts the ways of the old world. The poor and the despised, the prisoner and the captive, the sick and the near dead will have priority. The pious and the powerful may take offense at this; Jesus' Kingdom is not based on the goals of the old world — gaining status and power over others through education, precious careers, the things that we own. For this reason Jesus said that the prostitutes and the tax collectors will go into the Kingdom of God ahead of the religious elite, the scribes and the Pharisees (Matt. 21:31).

Theologians say that when Jesus talks about the Kingdom, he does so in two ways. He talks about it as present ("The Kingdom of heaven is at hand!") and future ("Thy Kingdom come..."). It doesn't seem that it can be both ways. Some claim that the Kingdom is not here yet, but that Jesus is describing what it will be like when it does come. Others say that Jesus brought the Kingdom with him and if we act right, then we can continue to bring it in. It does not have to be an either-or situation, though. Perhaps Jesus was trying to show that there is a tension between what is and what will be, between what we have done with our lives and what God will do with our lives, between the ways that we have tried to live in the old world and the way that we will live in the new Kingdom.

In the old world, unemployment will always be too high and bills will never be paid off. In God's Kingdom, however, all will be satisfied. The hungry will be fed; the thirsty will be given drink; the naked will be clothed; the dead will be raised to life. In the old world there will always be wars and rumors of wars; men and women will always be fighting. Someone will always be willing to step on another in order to get ahead. People will always be willing to take from another. But in God's Kingdom, the lion will lie down with the lamb, the abused of the world will be helped by good Samaritans, and the prince of peace will reign.

In the old world there will always be sickness; there will always be captivity; there will always be oppression. There will always be needle marks on people's arms. There will always be empty bottles that signify empty lives. In the old world death will forever reign. In God's Kingdom there will be freedom. Old death will be eclipsed by new life, because the Author of life will reign.

In the old world men and women will continue to live lonely lives forgotten by family and friends. Men will beat their wives and women will beat their children. People will die frightened and alone. But in God's Kingdom there will be the family of God. Brothers and sisters and mothers and fathers will live under the Father and Mother — God.

In the old world there is division. There are cliques and gangs. There are black and white. There are rich and poor. There are haves and have-nots. In the new Kingdom, though, there is no Jew or Greek, no slave or free, no male or female. There are no divisions. There is only the one family of God.

And Jesus spoke of this in tension. If he had spoken of it as only in the future, it would be pie-in-the-sky religion. If he had talked about it only in the present tense, heaven would be on earth, and we know that is not the case. The Kingdom is in tension in our lives. We can be members of the revolutionary group that Jesus started. We continue the revolution of the breaking in of the new Kingdom into the old world.

We begin by establishing the Kingdom in our own lives. Then we work for the liberation of those that live under the dictatorship of the old world. We show them that the Kingdom is coming and that we are already a part of it. We share the good news that there is room for them too. Regardless of the shape that they are now in, no matter what they are doing or what they have done, there is room. There is new life. We have the option to choose whether we will be a part of it!

"The presence of the Kingdom is quiet, unassuming, and consistent."

Part II

WORSHIP ON THE STREET

W<small>HEN</small> J<small>ESUS</small> <small>SPOKE</small> <small>OF</small> <small>WORSHIP</small>, he said, "Be careful not to do your 'acts of righteousness' before people, to be seen by them. If you do, you will have no reward from your Father who is in heaven" (Matt. 6:1). Jesus was referring to formal worship as he reminded people of what the basics were. "Acts of righteousness" took place in the Temple during structured worship activities. What had happened, though, was that everything was turning into a show. People would participate only so that they would be recognized. Prayers were long and flowing, but they said very little. The emphasis was on who put the most in the collection plate. The words of righteousness had superseded the acts of righteousness. Priorities were out of order.

"When, therefore, you give to the needy ..." (6:2). It is assumed that *everyone* gives money to the poor. That is an unconditional expectation of the Lord. Giving to those who are in need helps to remind the giver that he or she is not the center of the universe. We are reminded that the things that we own are not just for private use, but are to be shared. Giving to the poor helps, most importantly, to remind us that whatever we own is a gift. It was not earned, although we may have worked hard to obtain it. God gave it so others might be helped.

After people begin to share what they have with the poor, the second act of righteousness is learning how to pray. "And when you pray..." (6:5). Individual piety always is to follow communal activity, not the other way around! Too many of us have skipped the first act of righteousness to get on to the second. When prayer is divorced from practice, then all that is left are empty words and hollow action. People cannot know what prayer is until they do the things that naturally lead to prayer: Getting involved personally with the needy.

The problem that many of us have when it comes to matters of faith is that our priorities are out of order. We perform one without doing the other. But if we are involved with the needy, then our offering prayers will truly follow an offering. Our prayers for the sick will follow time spent with the sick. Our prayers of petition will come as the result of intervention that we as children of God have already made in the name of the Father. Then our prayers — and all our worship — will become full discussions with God of experiences that we have had trying to fulfill the mandate to share with the poor and to love our brothers and sisters regardless of their condition.

The third expectation mentioned is "And when you fast..." (6:16). Again it is assumed that we will fast. Just because most folks fast only when they wish to lose a few pounds does not mean that American Christians cannot identify with this third act of righteousness. Fasting is an outward expression of an inward condition. It is nothing more, or less, than giving up something for the Kingdom.

"Seek first the Kingdom and his righteousness and all these things will be added to you" (6:33). For too long, many Christians have allowed their worship to become little more than an outward show. Worship services are elaborate and flashy. Sermons are eloquent and flowery. Church buildings look more like museums than ministry stations. Service and commitment to the poor have taken a backseat to the other acts of righteousness. It is time for us to get our priorities back in order. An excellent place to begin is getting to know the poor — personally, just as Jesus said.

7

The Communion of Saints

The three of us chatted as we walked down the dirty sidewalk. Our conversation was interesting, our fellowship good, and the communion solid. But we did not really belong together as a group. On one side walked Bruce. A good ol' boy from the hills of North Carolina, Bruce had come to the big city a few years earlier. On his long road as a truck driver he had been through three marriages and too many jobs to count. Now he was a homeless alcoholic. The only thing that testified to his previous life was the tattoo on his arm: "Evelyn."

"Who's Evelyn?" I once asked.

"My third wife."

"Do you miss her?"

"She was a mean woman. She stabbed me once... yeah, I miss her."

Life is lonely on the streets.

Pouche was a tall, muscular black man from Boston. Once he got so angry that he tore a door off its frame because it was locked and he had no key. A handsome man, he too was a homeless alcoholic, although when he was not drinking it was impossible to tell. He recognizes the composers of symphonies when he hears them on the radio. He reads a great deal and can quote passages of Scripture at length. He can tell you virtually anything about St. Paul. And he is one of the hardest workers around. He became an alcoholic because he could never quite fulfill the high expectations that others always held for him.

I was a young white minister from the suburbs. Long hair and

35

ever in blue jeans, I had come to the city to receive the benefits
of higher education. A great deal of my time was spent within
the safe walls of an academic institution that did not require any
interaction with people so different from me. Yet here we were,
walking as friends. The only thing that could bring such different
individuals together was the power of Christ at work.

That night, walking and talking, the three of us discussed the
love of Jesus. A nigger, a red-neck, and a hippy preacher, all a
part of the family called the church that Jesus established.

We laughed and put our arms around each other. Continuing
to talk, we hugged one another and made our way in smiles to the
building. A man passed us by, pausing to look back at us. We
laughed at his perplexity. Bruce turned toward him and said, "It's
okay. We're not queer. We're Christian."

•

*Listen my beloved. Has not God chosen those who are poor in
the world to be rich in faith and heirs to the Kingdom which
he has promised to those who love him?*

[James 2:5]

•

O joyous God,

too often I stand before you as a joyless person, having forgotten
    what you have done for me, or not remembering the
    significance of your actions.

I go through life clutching at things rather than people, trying to
    hold onto all that I have and trying to obtain more than I
    need. Forgive me for that.

Too often, Lord, my praise is hollow noise.

    My prayers are empty words.

       My actions have only selfish motives.

          My life is a broken shell.

Yet, O God of joy, you have not forgotten me.

Your love still pours itself upon me to take if I will.

You still offer eternal life to me as I simply go through the
    motions of living.

You provide me with a church for fellowship and others who care
    about me when I don't care about myself.

You offer guidance,

    direction,

       purpose,

          love.

You offer joy.

Thank you.

Blessed be your name forever.

                                     Amen.

8

Hidden Talents

She looked very much like Olive Oyl in the cartoon strip except that her oily, stringy hair fell to her shoulders. Her name was Charlene and she came asking for food. With her were the babies. The oldest was into everything, and Charlene was always watching him make his mischief. She never said anything to him about it; she simply watched. Motherly instincts, in this case, were little more than detached observations.

The middle child was about two. He was quiet with oily blond hair and huge brown cow eyes. The rest of his body was small in comparison with his enormous head. His nose continuously drained onto his lip. Neither he nor his mother ever seemed to notice, although it drove nearly everyone else crazy. People would give Charlene tissues, which she would take and stuff into her oversized black purse. But she continued to talk without ever taking the hint.

The youngest was one. Already walking, this little boy never strayed far from his mother. He, too, had a nose that never ran dry. Whenever Charlene took the baby out of her lap, he would scream until she picked him up again.

As her application for food was being completed, Charlene continued talking (her mouth never ran dry either!). "Did I tell you that I play in a church. I mean I played piano in a church. I used to have a piano, but we had to sell it. You don't need a piano player do you?"

The church did need a piano player. Inner-city churches often have trouble finding people who can lead music. It was hard to believe, however, that "Olive Oyl" with the three babies could play the piano.

"Did you say you play the piano?"

Charlene didn't hear the question. She was already talking about something else. "So I left him and I took his television, too... er, What?" she asked.

"Do you really play the piano?"

"Yes. YES! I really do."

She talked as she walked down the hall to the sanctuary, as she sat down on the piano stool, as she opened the hymn book, and did not stop until she actually began to play. "I haven't played in quite a while now," she explained. "We had to sell our piano. Actually we could not take it with us. We had to leave in kind of a hurry. What do you want to hear? Oh, I know." And she began to play.

The familiar notes of the old hymn "He Lives" filled the room. It was magnificent. I could barely believe what I heard and saw. Olive Oyl was playing as well as anyone I had ever heard. She was solemn and serious as her fingers pressed the keys.

After a few moments, the middle child began to cry. Without missing a beat, continuing to play with only one hand, Charlene pulled down her blouse, scooped up the child so that he could suck, and then used both hands to play.

Finishing the hymn, she grinned broadly and said, "There. How's that?"

"You're hired," came the amazed reply.

●

...to one he gave five talents, to another two, to another one, to each according to his ability.

[Matthew 25:15]

●

O Lord,
sometimes I judge the talents of others wrongly.
Sometimes I prevent them from developing the talents you gave
    them.
Sometimes I think that I can do it better than anyone else, so I
    do it all!
Forgive me of my arrogance, Lord.
Remind me that I am a part of a team effort, your church, as we
    strive to serve you and others.
Remind me that even Jesus your son did not come as people
    expected him to. He was not dressed like a king. He did not
    speak like a king. He did not die like a king.
Do not let me forget, O Lord.
Make me a part of the people of God.
With others, let us develop the talents we have.

                                                            Amen.

9

Distracted Worship

That Sunday morning, the sanctuary was about three-quarters full. Everyone sang during the hymns — for a change. Usually only a few sing; most simply move their lips to the music. Larry is really the only one who cuts loose during a hymn. Whenever he is not in attendance it seems that no one sings. On those awful days it appears that everyone merely talks through the songs. (Responsive readings, on the other hand, are often spoken in a sing-song voice that makes them sound like hymns.) On this rare Lord's day, however, the singing, as well as the responsive reading, had gone well.

It was time for the special music. Inner-city churches often do not really have special music. Rather, they have a listing in the bulletin where special music would be if there were any — usually immediately after the offering.

Worshippers feel cheated when the preacher jumps up after the offering and launches into the sermon. "What happened to the special music?" they wonder, even though this has happened hundreds of times before. They grab their bulletins to make sure that it really says "Special Music." If it does, and it always does, they wonder what happened. By the time they reconcile themselves to the fact that there is no special music, the sermon is half over. On this day, however, there had been special music, and then everyone settled back to listen to the sermon.

The minister began with a funny story. They knew that they were being set up for the kill, but everyone likes a good story. They knew they should try to enjoy it, because in just a few minutes he would be stepping all over their toes. This is the kind of sermon folks like.

While everyone was listening, just as the preacher was about to step on the first toe, a roach began to crawl over the top of the third pew. He was half way across before anyone noticed. Charlene turned her eyes from the preacher to the roach. She watched intensely as the bug made its way past her toward the end of the pew. Just before the roach was out of her reach, she jerked her hand over, grabbed the bug, threw it to the floor with all her might, and stomped every bit of life out of the creature. All eyes moved from the minister to Charlene to where her foot had stomped the floor.

Charlene's eyes looked down to make certain that the roach was indeed dead. Then she settled back and fixed her eyes on the minister. He continued to preach as though nothing had happened. That Sunday was thereafter known as "Roach Sunday."

●

Praise the Lord!
Praise God in his sanctuary;
Praise God in the mighty firmament!
Praise God for the mighty deeds;
Praise God according to the exceeding gladness.
Let everything that breathes praise the Lord!
Praise the Lord!

[Psalm 150]

●

Lord,
too often my praise is not praise at all.
Rather, I show up at church just to see who else is there;
      to see what else is going on;
      to see if anything happens.
I do not come with an attitude of praise.
I do not come in a spirit of the servant.
I do not come as a participant, but as an observer.
Forgive me for that.
When it comes to my praise, O God, I am the most silent of
      people. Yet I really do want to express my thanks to you, my
      Lord, for the all benefits that come as a result of your
      relationship with me.
I promise that I will do all within my power to make my
      relationship with you a testimony to your greatness. When
      people see, O Lord, may they say that my whole life is a
      praise to the greatness of God.

                                                Amen.

10

The Would-Be Worshippers

I had been at the chapel since 6:00 A.M. After breakfast with the homeless, I had gone into my office to pray and meditate on that morning's message. During the Sunday School hour, I made my weekly walk around the building, and I ran across Fred, who wanted to attend services that morning. Fred was an alcoholic. He had recently been participating in our breakfast program. Each Sunday morning, the congregation made breakfast for the homeless and I had met Fred there. He had obviously been drinking over the weekend, but was now in the process of "coming down." Because of his intense desire to attend the morning service ("I really want to come, Rev!"), I told him that it would be all right for him to worship with us. He thanked me and took a seat by the aisle about three-fourths of the way back.

Just before the service, I began to make my way to the sanctuary. On the way down the hall, I encountered a man I did not know. He was quite drunk. I then remembered that it was "grape days" — the time around the first of the month when everyone has money and the wine flows. I inquired as to what he wanted, and he replied by saying that he wished to "praise God!"

I told him that I was sorry, but that when he drank he lost his right to worship with us. He protested as I escorted him to the door. "Whaddya mean I can't come?!" After I led him out, I made my way to the front of the sanctuary.

A few minutes after the service began, in walked the intoxicated would-be worshipper casting an angry, defiant glance toward me. During the first hymn, I walked to the back of the church and,

once again, escorted him to the front door. (Sometimes, I think
that inner-city churches need bouncers.) His protest grew louder
and angrier. "You're telling me that I can't worship when I want
to!"

"That's right," I replied. "You are too drunk to mean anything
that you're saying."

Back inside the sanctuary, I greeted the visiting church group
that was worshipping with us that morning. They were hoping to
help us as a mission project.

Later, during the second hymn, in walked the would-be worshipper again. He staggered down the aisle never taking his eyes
off of me. I immediately went to the back of the sanctuary and,
again, escorted him out. His protests were even more violent. He
cursed me and told me that no one could tell him that he could
not worship when he wanted to.

Back inside the sanctuary, I climbed behind the pulpit and
began the sermon. Ten minutes later, the persistent interloper
clumsily made his way to the second row and sat down. He threw
angry glares at me as I preached, while I attempted to give him an
intimidating stare.

Suddenly, he jumped up and, pointing a dirty finger at me,
exclaimed, "Why don't you ever tell the truth? You're not a man
of God. You're nothing but a...!" and he went on to tell the
entire church what his opinions were.

At once two church members who were sitting close by made
their way over to the man and began to escort him down the aisle
toward the door. One led him and the other pushed from behind.
The further away from me that he got, the louder his denunciations
grew.

And then up jumped Fred. Screaming out, he assumed a karate
position. The would-be worshipper turned red with rage, clenched
his fist, and yelled, "Come on! I'm ready to fight!" The two church
members turned white, as every eye was on the coming battle.

A third church member leaped up and over a pew, tackling
Fred, and in a moment all were out the door. Everything became
quiet as all eyes turned to me.

Returning their questioning stares, I picked up my sermon right
where I had ceased. I had no sooner begun to proclaim the good
news again, however, when an elderly woman stood up and began to speak. Wishing to make me feel better, she shouted out:

"Honey, don't you worry about it. Why I know how you feel. Just this morning, when I decided to come to church, I left a no-good drunk husband at home and as I was pulling out of the driveway I ran over the dog and knocked down the mailbox!"

The congregation burst into laughter and applause. Finally realizing that the sermon was over, I laid my head on the pulpit. The amusement of the fellowship continued. Looking up again, I saw that all were smiles — except the visiting church group, who sat shocked and stone-faced.

In jest, I asked them, "What would your pastor do in a situation like this?"

Laughter broke out again. But the visitors did not laugh. Then one solemnly rose and said in all seriousness: "Our pastor wouldn't be in a situation like this."

●

Blessed are you when men revile you and persecute you and utter all manner of evil against you falsely on my account. Rejoice and be glad, for great is your reward in heaven, for so people persecuted the prophets who were before you.

[Matthew 5:11–12]

●

Lord,

Is this what you mean?

Is this persecution for an American Christian?

Would my fellow brothers and sisters really not be here,
even if I needed them?

I don't think so. There are others who are being arrested for
proclaiming your good news. There are others who are
hungry to go to where people hurt. There are others who are
being crucified for you.

I just try to do what you want me to do.

I do the best that I can.

Sometimes, Lord, it seems that no one else understands.

Get me through these times, O Lord, when I feel alone.

Amen.

11

Communion Wine

It was a Wednesday afternoon, and I had stayed in the office to try to catch up on some work. Now it was time to head downstairs to the fellowship hall for the mid-week prayer service. Hearing some noise as I made my way down the steps, I paused to take a peek underneath to see if kids were hiding in the building again. Very often, inner-city churches cannot offer programs for children during worship services because they have so few traditional nuclear families. This means that few adults have any interest in assuring that there are worship opportunities for youth. As a result, during "adult" services, kids are always sneaking into the church.

Poking my head underneath the dim staircase, I found that the noise had not been made by children. Sitting alone was Bruce. Cuddled around a fifth of wine, he was singing softly to himself.

"Bruce," I asked. "What are you doing?"

Looking like a hungry puppy, he began to cry.

"Bruce, we're going to be having communion tonight, but we don't have any juice. Would you share your wine with the church? We need some communion wine."

He looked at the bottle and then he looked at me. Smiling, he proudly said, "Sure, Rev. Anything for the church," and he handed me the bottle.

Wine is the most precious possession to an alcoholic. Many will lie, steal, manipulate, and abuse another to get one more drink. There is no doubt that Bruce is an alcoholic, yet here he was, sharing his most prized possession with the family of God.

•

After taking the cup, he gave thanks and said, "Take this and divide among you. For I tell you I will not drink again from the fruit of the vine until the Kingdom of God comes."

[Matthew 26:27–29]

•

Lord Jesus,
when it comes to sacrificing for the sake of your Kingdom, I am
    not worthy to be called a co-heir to the throne.
I have made your supper nothing more than a symbol that you
    have commanded me to remember.
I do not look upon your actions that night as an example that I
    am expected to follow.
It is no wonder that the Kingdom seems so far off now.
I am unwilling to sacrifice the way that you sacrificed in an effort
    to bring the Kingdom into my life.
I make God share the throne of my heart with too many other
    gods, with too many other idols.
Forgive me for that, Lord.
I renew my commitment to your coming Kingdom.
I sacrifice all my life, and my life's possessions, for the purpose of
    furthering that Kingdom throughout the earth.

Amen.

12

Father's Day for the Fatherless

It was Dan's last Sunday with the church. A country-folk-rock singer with a Christian message, he had been a part of the church community for a few years. Now, however, he was following his dream to Nashville, where he hoped to make it big. We would certainly miss him. Dan filled a void by bringing his upbeat music to our inner-city fellowship.

He sang his music for us one last time. At the conclusion of the service, the church family decided to have a group prayer to send Dan off. As the heads were bowed and the eyes were closed, individuals began to pray one at a time.

After a while, Ralph cleared his throat. Ralph is an illiterate senior citizen from the neighborhood. He came to the church one Sunday morning a few years back as he was waiting for the bus in the cold outside the church building. As individuals made their way into the building for worship, they greeted Ralph. Eventually, he wandered in.

"Excuse me," he said. "Can I ask a question? I don't know how to catch the bus to get to church. Can I come to this church?" He was assured that he could, and he has been a part of the congregation ever since.

"Lord," he began. "I want to especially thank you for Dan. I was walking out of the church one Father's Day and he came up to me and put his arm around me and asked me where we were going. And I said, well, I don't know about you, but I'm going home to get something to eat. And he said, 'No you're not, Pop, 'cause I'm taking you out for Father's Day.' And he took me out, and I've thought of him as a son ever since, and it was the best Father's Day that I've ever had. Thank you, Lord. Amen."

There were tears in his eyes, and his voice cracked as he spoke. Dan, who was sitting next to him, reached over and held his hand. Someone said a final benediction, but no one was in a hurry to leave.

•

"I tell you the truth," Jesus said, "no one who has left home or brothers or sisters or mother or father or children or fields for me and the gospel will fail to receive a hundred times as much in this present age [homes, brothers, sisters, mothers, children and fields — and with them, persecutions] and in the age to come, eternal life. But many who are first will be last, and the last first."

[Mark 10:29–31]

•

Lord,

I am a blessed person.

Not only do I have a family, but I am a part of something larger:
    your family — the church,

men who are my brothers, women who are my sisters.

elderly people who are my parents and grandparents.

It is not a house that makes a home.

Shelter does not always provide security.

Blood relationships do not necessarily forge a family.

I thank you, O God, for the great gift of individuality, of the
    opportunity to be myself.

But, Lord, I pledge to remember that you have called me to be a
    part of a larger group,

to be an individual in community,

through the name of the Father of our family, his church.

                                                                Amen.

*"We just want ya to know that we love ya
and like the way ya play the guitar."*

THE SOCIETY
OF SALTY SAINTS
Matthew 10:1–4

Saint Peter? Saint Philip? Saint Simon? Saint Bartholomew? If we pause to consider the twelve apostles, we might not be impressed by their character. They were, according to most people's standards, not the sort of folk that preachers would pick to build a church upon. Yet, here they are — the foundations of the church!

There is no evidence that Jesus chose them because of their religious background. They did not seem to be brighter or nicer than other people. Quite the opposite, according to Frederick Buechner. When we read their story in the New Testament, we find "that they were continually missing the point, jockeying for position and, when the chips were down, interested in nothing more than saving their own skins. Their sole qualification seems to have been their initial willingness to rise to their feet when Jesus said 'Follow me' " (*Wishful Thinking,* Harper and Row, 1973, p. 62).

Or, as Anthony Campolo puts it: "When Jesus went to start the church where did he go? Did he recruit from the top scholars of the University of Jerusalem? Did he insist on scholarly expositors who thought they knew how to be relevant? Or did he pick up some fishermen who smelled bad, a couple of ex-prostitutes, and a midget named Zacchaeus? Face it — Jesus had a zoo on his hands. If Jesus had wanted people with credentials, he would have chosen the Pharisees. Instead, he took the people society said were nothing" (in *Metro-Ministry,* David Frenchak and Sharrel Keyes, eds. Cook Publishing, 1979, p. 31).

It's true that we never think of the twelve apostles in this way, but was not that one of Jesus' primary points? One reason that

54

Jesus was killed was because he continued to do things that most people never expected. It should be the same with the church if, indeed, it is still God's church. As Campolo concludes: "It seems startling...that in the face of this our middle-class mindset has opted for the pharisaical values that eventually nailed Jesus on the cross. When Jesus chose his leaders for his church he was more concerned about their potential to be surrendered to the Spirit than he was about their former training or background."

Perhaps we have gotten away from the agenda that Jesus had when he chose his crew and dispensed his job descriptions. Now, all too often, there are additional qualifications imposed before one can be a leader of the church. The pharisaical values that Jesus stayed clear from have made their way into too much of our thinking. All we need do, however, is take a look at the society of salty saints that Jesus formed to discover what the church is really about.

Saint Peter? Peter had a temper. On a bad day he would cuss out his brother, Andrew, for talking him into going into their father's fishing business. He would cuss out the manufacturers of his leaky old fishing boat. He would cuss out the people who worked for him because they worked too slow, then he would let them have it whenever they pulled ahead of him. He would even cuss out the fish for not biting or for biting too well. It's no wonder that later in his life he and Paul had so much trouble getting along. They were both hot-heads who wanted things their own way. Each was absolutely convinced, not so much that he was right, but that the other was wrong. Peter would scream and yell and bicker and threaten to make his point. He had all the makings of a great evangelist. He was a "Rambo"-style preacher — cutting everyone and everything down. People would be intimidated into joining the church movement.

For all his fire, however, there was an empty place inside him that he never quite got over. Late at night, when he was alone, the remembrance of painful words would ring in his ears: "Do you love me Peter?... Feed my sheep.... Before the cock crows three times you will betray me."

Then he would recall that Jesus told him he was a rock. At first, he probably thought Jesus was telling him that he had rocks for brains, but later he finally began to catch on to what was really meant. As Buechner puts it, "A rock isn't the prettiest thing in

creation or the fanciest or the smartest, and if it gets rolling in the
wrong direction, watch out, but there's no nonsense about a rock,
and once it settles down, it's pretty much there to stay. There's not
a lot you can do to change a rock or crack it or get under it's skin,
and, barring earthquakes, you can depend on it about as much as
you can depend on anything. So Jesus called him the Rock, and
it stuck with him the rest of his life. He could stop fishing for
fish, Jesus told him. He had been promoted. From there on out
people were to be his business" (*Peculiar Treasures,* Harper and
Row, 1979, p. 134).

Jesus knew that once people like Peter were committed to a
goal, they would spend the rest of their lives believing it, working
for it, and never resting until it came about. Peter was probably
a loner in his early days. He didn't like to get too close to other
people. That is why he came across so harshly. But then Jesus
told him to feed his "sheep." Peter had problems with the job the
rest of his life, but, he never quit trying.

Saint Philip? Here's one that would be right at home on the
"PTL Club." That is, if he could be tied down long enough. Philip
was into everything. He was one of those high-wired individuals
who never seems to slow down and is always rushing through one
thing so that he might get to another. It is amazing that he was
able to hang around Jesus for three whole years.

When it came to his religion, Philip might remind us of Arthur
Blessit, who goes all over the world carrying a huge, seven-foot
cross with wheels on the end. (Somehow I have a hard time imag-
ining Jesus' cross with wheels.) Dressed in blue jeans and a blue
shirt, Blessit walks down the streets of the world singing gospel
songs and preaching to anyone who will stop to ask him: "Excuse
me, but why are you carrying a cross with wheels on the end?"

Blessit's response is to quote the four spiritual laws, pass out a
pocket New Testament, throw a glass of water over their head
("McBaptism" — American style!), and lead in a few verses of
"Amazing Grace." As he walks off into the distance, carrying his
cross on wheels, Arthur can still be heard singing the fourth verse.

Philip must have been a lot like that. A burst of enthusiasm,
and before people knew what had hit them, he was gone. That
is what he did to his friend Nathaniel. "Come and see what I've
found," he told his friend. "I know where the Messiah is," he would
sing, "and you-oo-oo don't."

It was the same with a black man from Ethiopia he once encountered. After a quick course in New Testament interpretation, Philip baptized him, and before the Ethiopian had wiped the water from his eyes, Philip was gone. Here today gone today. He was so excited about evangelism that he never wanted to hang around for the nurturing of a community. So he didn't.

Saint Bartholomew? There are some who believe that Bartholomew and Nathaniel were the same person. A person with a name like Bartholomew likely changed it as soon as he was old enough. His childhood was plagued with his mother yelling out the back door, "Baaar-tha-laaa-meew!" His school chums probably picked up on it and, throughout school, kidded him about it — "Rumble, Rumble. Here come the cattle — Bartholomoooo!" The days of his youth were hell.

The apocryphal works that are said to be written by him all deal with hell and Jesus' going there. Given the torment of his youth, this is understandable. He was called a sissy. He was beaten up a lot. When he went to the beach, people kicked sand in his face. He was never elected president of anything. He never got the girl. He knew enough about hell to write about it.

Philip told him to come and see the Messiah. Having nothing to lose, Bartholomew did. He never stopped following. His name is mentioned only a few times (did the other disciples kick sand in his face?). He was a shy, quiet helper who chose to help by action rather than by a lot of talk. He was the one who stayed and washed the dishes after the Last Supper. He probably had a hard time fitting in, but he spent the rest of his days trying to.

Then there was Saint Simon. Luke calls him "the Zealot." He was a combination Mother Teresa and Malcolm X. Clarence Jordan once pointed out that Jesus must have spent many a night sleeping between Simon and Matthew. Matthew believed in self before country and, as a tax collector, he sold out his country to better himself. Simon was a patriot who believed in country before self and wanted to kill Matthew for being so selfish. Simon likely wore a flag button in his lapel, subscribed to *Soldier of Fortune* magazine, and belonged to the Moral Majority.

Not much is mentioned in the New Testament about Simon, probably because he spent all his time in secret meetings plotting the overthrow of the government that oppressed his beloved country. Any time there was a Roman in the crowd, Jesus had to make sure that someone kept an eye on Simon. During the invitation hymn, Simon was likely to slip up from behind and slit the Roman's throat.

Why would Jesus choose somebody like Simon to be an apostle? It doesn't make much sense. Unless it was to teach Matthew something. I would also guess that Matthew was chosen to teach Simon something. Simon could teach Matthew that some things are more important than one's own greedy desires. Matthew could teach Simon that love for one's country is not the most important thing in the world. They were two men starting out at opposite ends of the spectrum, but by the time Jesus finished with them, they ended up embracing one another and acting like brothers and working for the same purpose. I am sure they always had problems with each other, but the love that they had for Jesus made them continue to try to work things out.

Why did Jesus bring such a group of characters together? Why didn't he choose nice people who could carry on intelligent conversations? Why not choose folks who could carry out instructions without making a fuss? Why didn't he form a society of sophisticated saints? Instead, he began a society of salty saints who were questionable in character at best.

Perhaps it was because the church is in the world. The twelve represented all the crazy types of folks that make up this world that we live in. Most often, such different people hardly speak to, much less get along with, one another. We all have our own agendas. We all have our own feelings about how things should be. We all go our own way, often at the expense of others. That is what the twelve apostles were doing before they met Jesus. After they entered into a relationship with him, however, they not only began to get along; they also began to grow together, to learn from one another, and to love each other. By doing so, they began to mirror God's Kingdom on earth as it is in heaven.

> *For he is our peace who made us both one, and has broken down the dividing wall of hostility . . . that he might create in himself one person in place of two, so making peace, and might reconcile us both to God in one body through the cross thereby bringing the hostility to an end. . . . So then you are no longer stranger and sojourner, but you are fellow citizens with the saints and members of the household of God.*
>
> [Ephesians 2:14ff]

If the New Testament teaches anything, it emphasizes that there is no more vital bond than the oneness of those who are in Jesus Christ. If God's creation is going to be saved, if you and I are going to be saved, it will only be because we leave whatever philosophy or allegiance that we have been living by and become a part of the one mind of Christ Jesus. It is only the one mind of Christ that can save us from the evils of this world and the evils of our own hearts. His salvation is accomplished by us all in communion with each other.

People will think it odd, of course. We live in a world that expects us to maintain a proper distance between ourselves and other folks. Many are simply too suspicious of entering into this new way — this Christ way — of thinking.

"God can be seen in the streets and the alleys
if we will pause and look and listen....
Everyday people are the mouthpiece of God."

Part III

LESSONS FROM THE STREET

MANY FEEL THAT TO LEARN A LESSON FROM GOD, we must attend a church service, listen to a sermon, or participate in a Bible study. The struggle for faith and hope are readily seen, however, in day-to-day living. This is especially true of people who live in the inner city.

God can be seen on the streets and in the alleys if we will pause and look and listen. Too often we rush to and fro taking care of business — usually *our* business. We fail to see and to hear the many ways in which God is revealed. God has used the words of drunks, visions of poor mothers struggling to make ends meet, and the play of children in the streets to convey lessons for those who would follow the Kingdom. Everyday people are the mouthpiece of God.

If we take the time to observe these everyday events, we can be surprised. (Remember Jeremiah learned lessons from God while watching a man make a pot.) If we begin to use our eyes and our ears, God still has much to say.

13

"Doc"

Doc had turned the corner. For over a year he had been trying to overcome the disease of alcoholism that had dominated his homeless existence. After many monumental battles, it finally appeared that he was beginning to put it all together. The time that would lapse between drinking bouts was growing longer and longer. One day, he announced that it had been twenty-one days since he had taken a drink. Counting days is usually discouraged among alcoholics who are "on the wagon." After some time is built up, many find that they have good cause to celebrate — often by "falling off the wagon." Regardless, it had been twenty-one days since Doc had taken a drink, and he was proud of it.

He had become a regular at church services. He did not like to be formally recognized on these occasions, although he loved for people to notice that he was there. He beamed with pride when folks would shake his hand and tell him how good it was to see him in church.

There he would sit, talking the lyrics of the hymns, intensely forcing his eyes shut during the prayers, and hanging onto every word of the sermon. During the week, Doc would often ask questions regarding the sermon. "What does it mean to be a part of the family of God? What family? I ain't got no family. What does it mean to ask Jesus to come into my heart? A heart is just a muscle that pumps pain." He always listened. He always wanted to know.

Many of the people that Doc brought to church with him had already joined. He never came alone; he always "compelled" others to come worship too. The group sat together, somewhat separated from the rest of the congregation. It was usually obvious that they had slept outside the night before. Their clothes were dirty, and even though they had cleaned up the best they could in the bathroom sink, their skin was red and chapped from the cold.

Their red noses and their red eyes were enough to tell that they were different from other church folks.

Doc had learned the names of many of his fellow worshippers, and he loved to call people by name whenever someone spoke to him. "Love ya!" he would say. It seemed that he was well on his way to becoming a part of the Christian community.

On a Wednesday night he sat with his friends in a fast food hamburger joint. They were doing what most street people do — drinking coffee, not saying much of anything, trying to stay inside. "When you live on the streets you run out of things to talk about," Doc once said. "The past is just a mindful of memories that mean nothing to no one." The homeless often blame themselves for their situation, and so there is no reason to talk about families, friends, and life from the days before they became destitute. So they simply sit and wait.

The manager of the chain did not like "that kind of people" trying to weather out the long nights inside his restaurant. Recently, he and the managers of other such establishments had passed a rule that customers could remain for only half an hour after they finished their order. Homeless people, who usually just ordered coffee, could stretch this into an hour and a half when they could get refills.

On this night, however, their time was up. Doc and his friends saw the manager "giving them the eye," so they got up to leave. Suddenly, Doc stumbled and fell. His companions, used to alcoholic blackouts, tried to make him comfortable on the clean white floor. The manager, looking on in disgust, picked up the phone and began to dial the number of the police. The servers kept right on serving. Hungry customers continued eating. On this night, it did not matter to Doc. He was dead. He died right after he had turned the corner.

•

Jesus replied, "Foxes have holes and birds of the air have nests, but the Son of Man has no place to lay his head."

[Luke 9:58]

•

Lord Jesus,
it is an urgent gospel that you have entrusted to us.
I have an obligation to go wherever I might so that the poor have
an opportunity to receive good news,
so that prisoners can hear freedom announced;
so that the blind can recover their sight;
so that the oppressed might be released from whatever oppresses
them.
You have charged me with the task of helping to bring these
things about, Lord.
You want *me* to proclaim your acceptable year?
Lord, I have not even lived an acceptable day!
Yet, O God, I know that there are hundreds upon thousands who
need a little good news now!
They may not have the opportunity tomorrow.
It is true that I may not have much good news, but I do have a
little.
It may not make much difference, but, then again, it might.
I pledge it to you and to my hurting brothers and sisters.
Take what I share, O Lord, and make it into what is needed,
Through the Lord who can multiply loaves and fishes so that the
hungry can be fed.

Amen.

14

Lost in Love

She sat quietly in the waiting area of the bus terminal. Her solitude was in stark contrast to everything else in the room. The place, as always, was packed. Military men and women watched the small television sets that are a part of the chair that they slept in. At least fifty children were gathered around the video games that occupied one corner of the huge room. The games were turned up very loud so that their noise dominated the rest of the cacophony. Many families and couples were huddled throughout the room as they tried to say good-bye or hello to loved ones. Virtually every seat was taken. A murmur of endless chatter was the only sound that competed with the endless bleeps, screeches, and blasts of the video games.

The level of the noise and the large number of people made her look all the lonelier. Everything that she owned was stuffed into the three bags that lay at her feet, cluttering up the aisle. As people stepped over her possessions, they would remark that they were in the way or they would shoot her a look of utter disgust.

She took no notice of them as she continued to feed her four-month-old baby. She had to be careful, as she had only a few more of the sample bottles of baby milk that the hospital had given her, and it was going to be a long bus ride home.

Home? She had left a few months earlier with her new husband. "We were in love," she explained. The love that they held for one another manifested itself in the fact that she was very pregnant. Her parents were outraged that she could have been so stupid. "There are ways," they screamed, "to keep these things from happening! Look what you've done to your life!" She must have heard it a thousand times. She did not really seem to mind this though. For she knew that she loved him and that he loved her. She was going to have a new family in the place of the one that did not seem to understand. So when he suggested that they hitchhike somewhere to make a new beginning, she was ready to go build their new life together.

Now, however, she was going back home to the "I told you so's" of her parents. Somehow, things had not worked out the way she had planned. The baby was born in Nashville. They stayed in the Mission except for the time that she was in the hospital. He had tried to find work, but there were thousands of others looking for work in the music city as well. He just couldn't find anything that would pay enough to take care of the three of them. Someone told them that there was work up north so daddy, mama, and the baby made their way up I-65.

They met a friend in Louisville who invited them to stay with him for a few days until dad could find some work. Although he looked, he very quickly discovered that things were just as difficult as they had been in Nashville. The few days that they stayed with the friend soon turned into a few weeks. Finally, he told them that they had to leave.

They stayed at the Salvation Army. Then they stayed outside. Finally, they were back at the hospital waiting room. The baby had caught pneumonia. It was there that he told her that she ought to back home until he could find work. As soon as he found something, he promised, he would send for her. She protested, of course. They were in love, she said. After many tears, he conceded that it was just a crazy idea. "Never mind," he said.

The next morning, however, he was gone. She did not know where. She waited as long as she could, but the hospital was ready to discharge the baby and there was nowhere for her to go. After a while, she concluded that he was looking for work. She should go home as he had said. She knew that he would send for her later. They were, after all, in love.

•

*Love is patient and kind; love is not jealous or boastful; it is
not arrogant or rude. Love does not insist on it's own way; it
is not irritable or resentful; it does not rejoice at wrong, but
rejoices in the right. Love bears all things, believes all things,
hopes all things, endures all things. Love never ends. . . .*

[1 Corinthians 13:4–8]

•

Lord of love,
There are so many times that I have cheapened love in my life. I
    have used the words when I really did not mean them. I have
    said that I loved so that I would not have to act. I have
    claimed there was love when there was none.
I pray for forgiveness. I have contributed to the false love that
    dominates the lives of so many of your children — my
    brothers and sisters.
I pray for wisdom to distinguish feelings of true love from other
    feelings that I sometimes mistake for it.
I pray for courage to love in the way that you intend your
    children to love.
I pray for consistency so that the love that I offer will not be
    wishy-washy and shallow.
I pray that my life will be dominated by the example of love that
    was set by your son, my Savior, when he walked upon the
    face of the earth.
Through the name of him whose every action was an example of
    a life that was lived for love's sake,

Amen.

15

The Faces of Jesus

Chester is a sixty-five-year-old alcoholic. He was born and raised in the same city. He worked as a nurse's aid for a number of years and his future seemed bright. Then he began to drink. The drinking became serious after a while so that, he later said, "Before I knew what had happened, I had to have a drink to get started and I had to have one to end up." As a result he found that he could no longer hold down a job.

With little income, Chester found himself with few options in life. His family tried to help, but found him difficult to work with. "If you would just quit drinking," his sister often told him, "we would be able to help you out. Then you could put things back together again." As the grade-school story of Humpty Dumpty teaches, however, once broken, life is very hard to put back together again.

It wasn't that Chester did not try. "One time," he said, "I quit six times in one day!" Soon his family would have little to do with him. Not caring to sleep in a mission house, claiming that "they treat you like cattle," he slept outside. And, despite his efforts to quit, he continued to drink. Often he would go to his sister's back porch to sleep at night. Being an early riser, he was always gone before anyone knew that he had been there.

One day, however, Chester finally decided that he had had enough. He began attending an out-patient alcohol treatment program, and he began to attend church. At the church breakfast for the homeless, Chester would announce to the crowd the current status of his battle with alcohol. "I haven't had a drink all day!"

he would proudly announce, but it was hard for anyone to get excited at eight o'clock in the morning. After a few months, however, the hours without a drink had turned into days and the days into weeks.

His involvement with the church also grew. One Sunday morning, he made a profession of faith and joined the church. He asked if he could move into an unused Sunday School room. In return, he would become chief cook and bottle washer. He began to cook a Wednesday evening meal for the entire church, and he operated a clothing closet for street people. He began to minister to others as he had been ministered to.

Once Chester was asked to address a large gathering of church folks. Standing before them in the brown suit that he had obtained from the clothes closet that morning, he told them: "People ask me all the time how I was able to quit drinking after forty-five years. They want to know how someone like me can spend his time cooking food for others, giving out clothes, studying my Bible. Well, it was easy. I found Jesus. I had heard about him for a long time. I heard he was in the Bible or in some church or another. Sometimes I would go looking for him in those places, but I never found him. Then one day I stumbled across him. He was in the faces of the people at the church. I knew right then that I wanted to be a part."

•

"Beloved, if God loved us, we ought also to love one another."
                                                            [1 John 4:11]

•

Lord of love,
I have taught myself to survive in this life.
I have learned the tools of survival;
I keep my feelings to myself;
I play it cool;
I never talk to strangers.
I cherish privacy and honor the formalities that provide
    protective distance between me and others.
I do not trust other people.
That is not living Lord.
This is protecting myself just in case I stumble across some life.
This is not the way that you intended things.
I pause to thank you for my friends and acquaintances who take
    the initiative to get me off dead center and draw me a little
    further outside myself.
Most of all I thank you for your self-disclosure in Jesus, your son.
    In his life, I see how things were intended. Through him and
    my brothers and sisters, help me to make my way back,
    however painful the trip might be, into your intentions
    regarding my life.
Through the name of the one whose entire life was love.

                                                        Amen.

16

Lament

Sharon died on the Friday before Thanksgiving. The church received a call just before she died from the hospital social worker who was trying to track down her closest relative. Sharon had listed the name of the church under next of kin. She had a father somewhere, but nobody could remember where. She had married someone named Tex, but they had stayed together for only a few weeks.

By the following Monday, no one had claimed the body. The father never answered his phone. Tex was just a name. No one had expressed any interest in her burial. It appeared that she was going to be buried in Potter's Field by county employees. The church wished that it could have done something, but no one knew what. No one had the money to pay for a proper funeral. As it was, there was no service to attend. Burials by the county are not accompanied with a service.

People in the church had known about her illness for a while. Many had intended to go by and visit. Few ever did, though. Things just kept coming up. Life kept getting in the way. There are so many things that must be done around a church. Before anyone knew it, Sharon was dead.

In the church office, on the Tuesday before Thanksgiving, an impromptu memorial service was held. People began to recall their memories of Sharon.

"I first met her in front of the church building. I don't really know that much about cars so I was really just fooling around with mine. It was a cool fall Saturday. Sharon and the man that she was living with walked by. He was black. She was white. I peeked out from under the hood.

"'Hello,' I said smiling.

"They walked on by. A few moments later, however, they were back. I spoke again. They stopped. I stopped."

"'You know,' she began, 'nobody much speaks to us. Why did you?'

"'I don't know. Just trying to be nice.' I really couldn't believe that they had asked such a question. I thought it must have been because she was white and he was black.

"'We want you to know,' she said, 'that we appreciate it.'"

After a while, Sharon began to attend church services. The church soon discovered that she and the black man were no longer together. It was at the church that she met Tex, though. He was a homeless drifter from rural Kentucky. They sat together and, before anyone knew it, they announced that they were married. Both claimed that they wanted to straighten out and make a happy life together. They began by making professions of faith and joining the church.

The new lives quickly became old, however. Tex went to jail for something. Sharon went back to "old ways" and began to drink. She came to church only occasionally. Church members tried to talk sense to her, but she was always in too much of a hurry to listen.

All too soon, she died. The medical explanation was liver disease brought about by excessive drinking. Some church people say that it was because she couldn't survive the life that she had made for herself. Others claimed that she never really wanted to change at all, but was trying to take the church for a ride.

Still others claim that she died of a lifetime of broken hearts. A few just know that she is dead and that they miss her.

•

And behold, some who are last will be first, and some first will be last.

[Luke 13:30]

•

Lord of life,
I recall some whom I have come into contact with who are now
  departed from me.
I sought to speak a kind word to them.
I tried to be their friend.
But Lord, they did not receive me.
Or my words fell on deaf ears.
Or they had no need of my friendship.
Are these failures?
Are they seeds that you are growing?
I am bothered, Lord.
I wish to see results of my efforts and I see none.
Lead me to live in your vision.
I am blind.

              Amen.

17

The Three-Dollar Man

He was a plump, little, silver-haired man in his mid-fifties. Rosco was also homeless, often choosing to live outside rather than in one of the missions. Originally from Georgia, he was always talking about going home. Nobody believed that he would, though. There was nothing in Georgia for him to go home to. All his family had died or disappeared. "If I just had a few dollars tucked away somewhere," he would say, "then I'd get off of these damn streets and go back home." Aside from the state of his origin, nobody really knew much about Rosco. Because he was so pleasant to have around, everyone liked him.

He was beaten to death in a robbery for the three dollars that he had in his pockets. It was the first of the month and the drinking cycle had begun on the streets. Whenever a new month begins, homeless men and women receive pension checks, social security checks, or retirement checks. Many of these recipients are alcoholics, and their money pays for wine. "Grape Days," that time when the wine flows freely on the streets, usually last until the second week of the month. If anyone has any money left, even if it is only a few dollars, that person is wealthy.

Word on the street, which is usually reliable, was that Rosco must have flashed his money. He was beaten with brass knuckles for a long time. With blood oozing out of his mouth and cuts on his face, he somehow made his way to the church. The emergency medical service was called. It took thirty minutes for them to arrive. The paramedics looked Rosco over for a long time.

"Does he have insurance?" one of them asked.

No one at the church knew whether he did or not.

"What has that got to do with anything?" demanded an angry neighbor.

The paramedics talked to one another for a while. Finally, they informed the church that there was little reason to take Rosco to the hospital as he just needed rest. Someone could take him to see a doctor later. They said to call if there were any problems. After patting Rosco's hand and assuring him that everything would be fine, they left.

A short while later, Rosco began throwing up blood. Someone tried to call the paramedics again. "I should have gone home," coughed Rosco. A few moments later, he died.

●

But let justice roll like waters, and righteousness like an ever flowing stream.

[Amos 5:24]

●

Lord of life,
selfish greed too often triumphs in this life.
When it is so flagrant,
I am too angry to pray.
I am too mad to cry.
I demand action!
Your action!
My action!
Yet, there is nothing done.
Injustice prevails.
Life is cheapened for another's gain.
So while I wait on the deliverance of the Lord,
I placidly carry on with life.
Yet, my walk is a little slower,
as my feet drag in the dust.

Amen.

18

One Christmas in the City

Holidays are the worst time for the homeless. While everyone else is gathering with their families to shoot fireworks, carve turkeys, or open presents, street people just hang around and wait until the festivities are over. Sometimes, of course, church groups or civic-minded people sponsor a dinner for the homeless on Thanksgiving or Christmas, but it is rarely anything more than an institutional meal served after a prolonged prayer by someone dressed in a Santa suit. Soon after the meal is over, street life returns to normal. The group goes home to celebrate their good deed with their families. The homeless sit around and wait for the rest of the day to pass. It is little wonder that the destitute drink more during the holidays than at any other time.

But one Christmas was different. The street people who hang around the church decided to get involved. Because no one else wanted to, a few of the "guys" volunteered to construct a manger scene for the annual Christmas pageant sponsored by the church's young people. By the time they had finished, over twenty uprooted individuals had helped with the project.

It was a simple wooden stable that was stained a dark maple. Some of the wood that they used was bad, but that gave the three-sided structure a realistic look. The manger sat in front of the pointed-roofed stable. It was a simple V-shaped trough supported by four straight legs forming X's.

Some of the men had walked to the stockyard ten blocks away to obtain hay. They returned dragging two huge boxes. The smell of a barnyard was overwhelming.

"That stinks," someone said.

"Well," explained one of the men, "we brought back two kinds of hay. One box has clean hay and the other has, uh...not so clean hay."

"Why in the world did you bring used hay?"

"We didn't know how realistic you wanted to make it," came the stone-faced reply.

The clean hay was scattered around the front of the church. One of the men pulled out a can of red spray paint. After shaking it up, he began to paint across the back of the stable, "R.C. was here."

Some of the other men, who were proud of their work, complained that he was messing everything up. They took the paint away from R.C., demanding an explanation.

"Well," began R.C., "if Jesus were going to be born today in a modern-day stable, you can bet that it would have graffiti all over it." No one argued with his logic, but they covered the paint job with more stain.

The finishing touch to the scene was the star that someone had cut out of cardboard and covered with tin foil. Standing on one another's shoulders, they suspended the star from the roof of the sanctuary so that it hung almost over the stable. Standing back, they put their arms around each other and admired their work.

When we performed the pageant a few days later, street people came for the first time. They sat on a pew close to the front. They smiled broadly and sang along when the carols were sung. They shut their eyes when the prayers were prayed. They carefully watched the weary Mary and Joseph travel to *their* manger. They observed the birth of the baby Jesus and saw the shepherds come to worship and the kings that brought gifts. They heard the angels sing of joy to the world.

When the pageant was over, they were slow to leave. "This sure has been a good Christmas, hasn't it?"

"Yeah. For a change, it sure has been. I wonder why?"

"I don't know, but I can't wait until next Christmas."

"I know what you mean. I hate to see this one end."

•

And Mary said, My soul magnifies the Lord, and my spirit rejoices in God my Savior, for he has regarded the low estate of his handmaiden....

[Luke 1:46]

•

Lord Jesus,

at times during the year our lives are full of bright lights and gay, happy music;

there are Santas in the stores and light beaming from children's faces;

when they see him they stare in awe and wonder.

The familiar sounds of ringing bells abound.

Choirs sing,
    children laugh,
       shoppers shop,
          givers give,
             the world is merry and bright.

Yet, O God, when we see beyond the bright lights and the gay music, we can see other things.

We can see the worried faces of parents who do not yet know if Santa will come to their house.

We see the elderly waiting alone, in desperate hope that there will be more than a token visit from their family.

We see men and women trying to numb the pain of being alone by drinking alcohol or by injecting drugs.

We see children who will compare what Santa brought them with what he left others, and they will painfully realize that Christmas, like life, is not always fair.

We can see the many who are dull-eyed and empty-faced with the feeling that there is nothing to celebrate.

O God, the pain of such irony is overwhelming to us who want to remember that Christmas is your birthday.

Give us compassion this Christmas, so that we will pray for those who have nothing and those who feel nothing, so that we will be moved to action.

Give us the power to give without attaching strings to our gifts.

Give us the desire to share the knowledge of what Christmas is really about.

Most of all, give us the love of Christ,

so that we can give it to others during this holiday time,
for that is the best way that we can celebrate your birthday.
In the name of the baby born in poverty
so that we might be rich beyond all that has ever been imagined.

Amen.

"*Jesus inverts the ways of the old world.
The poor and despised, the prisoner and the captive,
the sick and the near dead will have priority.*"

PROMISES IN
THE WILDERNESS
Hebrews 3:1–16

We had been friends for a long time. We had cried together. Laughed together. Dreamed together. And by either calling or coincidence we were a part of the same profession. On this particular Friday morning we felt every bit like the ministers that Paul describes in 1 Corinthians 4: "... the dregs of humanity...." After staying up much too late the night before, we somehow arose early enough to begin our pilgrimage.

In the car we talked about our dreams and our convictions. We discussed the things that we believed in and the theological ramifications of the incarnation of the said propositions. Then we discussed baseball.

Down a long and winding road lined with pecan trees and peanut plants we drove. We rode past the Rehoboth Baptist Church, and finally we arrived.

The mystic on the mountaintop whom we sought turned out to be a white-haired lady wearing galoshes. "Come help me bear my load," she said. We gladly did. Through the tall, wet grass she led us to her home. On a screened side porch the journey began. It lasted for quite a few hours, interrupted only by the fellowship of the meal and the pouring of iced tea. There were long periods of silence as we let her words of wisdom sink into concrete heads.

"But Mrs. Jordan, what if...?" we asked.

"What of my family...?" we needed to know.

"Yet there are friends I love who...," we implored.

"But our situation is different...," we tried to make her understand.

And she listened with kind patience. She smiled. She told us story after story of families and friends and different situations and what if's. She led us through the "valley of the shadow of doubt" and to the mountaintop ecstasy of faith. She offered her shoulder to cry on. She shared freely a lifetime of experiences. She told us that above all we are to take the commands of her Master seriously.

But that was precisely the problem. This was our difficulty. This was the reason that we had come. We do take them seriously. We have a glimpse of what could happen if we take them seriously. Her very life is a testimony to what happens to people who take the words of the Master seriously — all hell breaks loose! Economics is turned upside down. Losers become winners. The powerful are pulled down from their positions. The possessors become the possessed and the captured are set free. The poor are made rich and the rich are made poor. And it is Jesus himself who stands in the very middle.

This is why we were there. How in the world could a sane human being stand up for such things? We didn't know and we felt like we were supposed to. How are we to be Christians? We are not even sure if we know what a Christian is anymore. How in the world are we to take all the promises of the Master seriously?

> *If you would take him seriously today,*
> *don't let your souls get calloused, like they did that day in*
> *   the wilderness,*
> *when I got sick and tired of their demands for proof;*
> *when your fathers and mothers tried my patience with their*
> *   "let's-be-practical" speeches,*
> *and were given forty years in which to see plenty of my*
> *   "Proof."*
> *So I got thoroughly fed up with that bunch and I said,*
> *"They are eternally making a mess of things*
> *simply because they pay no attention to my instructions."*
> *While in this upset condition I swore*
> *that they would never achieve my rest.*
>
> [Hebrews 3:3–11, CPV]

The speech of God in the third chapter of the book of Hebrews spoke to my situation. Here I was in my wilderness, just as many others are when it comes to their faith. It is a time when we desperately need to hear a word from the Lord. We want God to speak to us directly. We want Jesus to become real to us. And we are wandering through the wilderness of our lives hoping to bump into God. But we find that our souls are getting calloused. We are ever demanding signs of proof. We are forever delivering "let's-be-practical speeches" to both God and ourselves.

Could it be that God is unreal to us because we have lapsed into the same condition that the Hebrew children did after God had already led them through the greatest liberation of all time? Could it be that God is saying the same things about you and me? Is it you and I who have calloused souls? Is it you and I who are demanding signs of proof? Is it you and I who are trying to be both realistic and "Christian" at the same time? Could it be that God is saying about you and me: "They are eternally making a mess of things simply because they pay no attention to my instructions?" And as a result, is it you and I who will never find God's rest?

Well, we certainly haven't found it yet, have we? How many of us are satisfied? How many have found God's rest? How many are hurting? How many lonely? How many losing the battle over addiction? How may suffer from broken relationships? How many from lack of purpose? How many are there who are able to live consistently the things that they say they believe in? How many are there here who are caught up in an American rat race and who don't know how to get out? How many are there who are possessed by their possessions? How many are possessed by desire for them? How many are there who have not grown weary of the search for God's rest and our liberation? How many here are there who have given up completely the search for God? How many church members are there who have calloused souls? How many have become calloused people? How many calloused Christians?

I believe that the majority are still searching, still looking to get closer, still finding that they are nowhere near where they think that they should be, and are still hurting. Too many who are "professional helpers" find that they are burned out and tired after all the helping. Soon we all begin to wonder if we make any difference at all. Then, too many find that we are losing in the battle for a good and fulfilled life.

Why? How could this be? We have prayed before. We have asked God to come into our lives and take away evil desires or to heal us or to make our lives better somehow. Most of us do not feel as if our prayers were answered.

We merely go through the motions of discipleship. Others of us have committed ourselves to making a difference. We believe in the things that the Bible calls us to attain — the right of all God's children to live in dignity, the right for every person to have a decent job, justice, peace, and all the other goals that stem from the Bible. We work hard to feed, to clothe, to house, to establish justice where there was none, to find the path to peace, and so on. It is not just our neighbor, but the whole world that needs to be saved.

But we find that everything that we do never seems to be enough. There are always more who need help, more who need peace, more who need to be set free, more who need . . . us. We recoil in fear that if we give ourselves totally to all who need us, there would be nothing left for us. There are others who hope to find food, fellowship, freedom, understanding, and even God. Still others have given up worrying. These feel that they will simply do what they can do and leave it at that.

There is still the hope, however, that the living, resurrected Jesus will one day become just as real to us as he was to women in a garden or fishermen in a boat. Why do we hope? Why do we commit ourselves? Why do we pray for change? Why are we all searching for more fulfillment out of life than we currently have? Why, in spite of all our trying, do we still find that we cannot overcome the things that hold us down? That oppress us? What keeps us going? What makes people still hang around churches? Why are alcoholics still around years after they began to think about quitting drinking and giving their lives to the Lord? What keeps lonely people coming to church looking for fellowship? What keeps hurting peoples coming to look for healing? What gets folks through another day — even when they don't have the desire to make it through another minute?

I think that it is because the God who is involved in our lives is a God who has made some promises. In the early history of the Bible, God made a promise to Abram. If the old man would leave behind everything that he had come to trust in and live the rest of his life going wherever God led him, then God would start a new nation, in a "promised land," and the old man himself would become a blessing to countless people.

When the Israelites were oppressed as slaves in the land of Egypt, God intervened and liberated them from their oppressors.

And God promised that they would be led to a new land — a "promised" land — if they could only learn to depend on nothing but God.

In the time of the first church, Peter preached to the crowd at Pentecost, and he said: "Repent and be baptized, every one of you in the name of Jesus the Messiah for the forgiveness of your sins; and you will receive the gift of the Holy Spirit. For the *promise is to you,* and to your children, and to all who are far away, every one whom the Lord our God will call" (Acts 2:37–39).

In this time when so many of us are wandering around in the wilderness of our lives, we might pause and know that the same promise that was made to Abram, the Israelites, and the people of the first church is also made to us. If we place all our trust in God and practice the teachings of Scripture, then the love of the Lord will become real in our lives; then we will meet the resurrected Jesus face to face.

What is faith? Clarence Jordan offered a good definition: "Let me tell you that faith is not a theoretical belief. I would go further and say that faith is not a stubborn belief in spite of all evidence. That is not faith. That is folly.... Faith is not a belief in spite of evidence, but *a life in scorn of the consequences!*" (*The Substance of Faith and Other Cotton Patch Sermons,* Association Press, 1972, p. 42). Faith isn't so much what we think as it is what we do! Abram thought that he was half crazy for leaving behind the comforts and security of everything he knew to follow a God who made a promise — the substance of which was "I'll be with you!" The children of Israel thought that they had lost their minds when they left behind their oppression for a life in the desert. At least their oppressors had fed them. Out in the desert they would have no one to rely on but God; surely they would need more than that! The people of the first church knew that a decision for Christ could cost them their very lives. They felt that they were committing suicide when they walked up to Peter and the other disciples to tell them that they were going to join them. All of these people acted on *nothing more than a promise* that things could be better than they are now.

And in each case God made good on the promise. Abram became Abraham and found that he was taken care of. The children of Israel ate bread that fell from heaven and survived the wilderness and even made it to the "promised" land. The people of the first church found forgiveness, community, and a living Jesus who was as real to them as the stars over their heads and the dirt under their feet. It was all because they acted in spite of the consequences. They acted in spite of how they felt. They even acted in spite of their doubts. *And when they acted, God acted.*

Not much has changed in the way that God deals with people. If we act, God acts. If we continue to practice the principles of the Promised One, then God will continue to act in a way that is real to us. This is God's promise to us. The power of a promise is often power enough to move individuals and peoples to work toward a new life, a new community, and a new world — by implementing the ways of God and a new world.

After we left the white-haired saint who wore galoshes, there was one additional thing that I had to do. I wanted to go and see the shack where her husband, Clarence Jordan, had spent his evenings writing. He had translated the Cotton Patch Gospel and had written all his sermons in the little place. It was here, while translating the ninth chapter of the Gospel of John, that Clarence had died. It was a little one-room aluminum shack that stood in the middle of a corn field. I wanted to see it because I hoped to capture some of the feelings that he must have felt. I wanted to stand in the place where he had wrestled to know God.

When we got to the shack I was disappointed to see that it had not been kept up. Weeds grew wild all around it. It was dirty. The screen had rotted off the front door. This was not the way that I would have treated such a "holy" place. I walked in ahead of Greg, our guide, and Guy, my friend. Inside there was only clutter. Discarded paper from an adding machine lay on the floor. Dirt and spider webs were everywhere. An old, worn-out easy chair took up almost half the room. It was in a reclined position as if someone had quickly jumped from it and hadn't put it back in place.

I had stood there for only a moment, surveying the scene, when I felt something prick my back. I turned and felt it again. "Wasp!" yelled my guide and my friend. I ran and scratched my back and felt both the wounds and the disappointment. Holy places should be... holy. As I walked away, however, I found myself thinking. Perhaps God, or maybe even Clarence, was trying to say to me, "Get out of here! Go back out there! Go back where everybody else is! Don't come in here to think. You've already had all day for that. Now it is time to go turn your dreams into deed."

Sticking my head in that empty shack was much like sticking my head inside an empty tomb — there was nothing there. So I left that day. I knew that I had things to do. I had a God to follow whose promises I trusted. And I had a life of faith to live. I left knowing full well that our God is not a God of empty tombs, cold shrines, or even wordy liturgies. Our God is a God of action. And God is waiting for us to join the action.

"The greatest theological truths grow out of the struggles that make up everyday lives."

Part IV

WORD ON THE STREET

ATLANTA COLUMNIST LEWIS GRIZZARD tells the story of a preacher who once came to town to conduct a tent revival. "The end is close at hand!" he screamed one night. About that time, a small boy who had been given a toy trumpet for his birthday walked past the tent and gave his new horn a mighty toot.

The congregation panicked and bolted from the tent. The evangelist grabbed the cash box and cut down the street at full gallop. To find out what was going on, the little boy followed.

The preacher ran faster and faster afraid to look back, but the little boy matched him step for step, tooting the horn all the way. Finally the preacher stopped, whipped out a switchblade, and said, "Watch it, Gabe, or I'll cut you good!"

Too many of us are like the preacher — talking biblical idealism, but rarely willing to show that we will pay the price to make these ideals a reality.

Good proclamation seeks to take the ideal out of the Bible and place it in the lives of the hearers. Jesus never intended for sermons to become mere expressions of meaningless idealism. We are told to be doers of the word and not hearers only (James 1:22).

19

The System of Denial

They came to the church because they had heard of the social services that were provided. The church raised money to help pay utility bills, purchase medicine, and buy other things that they might need but were unable to obtain. One of the volunteer social workers had told them over the phone that, if they raised all but $15 of their $185 water bill, the church might be able to help with the rest.

As they worked hard to raise the $170, the church helped others with $15 here, and $25 there, assisting people to keep their heat on, baby food on the shelf, prescriptions filled, and clothes on their backs. The lower the chapel's social service account got, the closer they came to reaching the unreachable.

Finally, the money ran out before the end of the month. The chapel had no more funds with which to assist people. In the end, the account was such that no one else could be aided.

Then they came to see us. "We've raised all but $15," she said with a broad, proud grin. "We can keep our water on."

Janice, the social service worker who exhausts all possibilities to help people in need, got up and walked over to the counter. Slowly, she said, "You're going to think this is funny." Then she started to laugh. It was a forced, sad laugh.

As she laughed, echoes of laughter came from the other side of the counter. Together the trio laughed. They laughed out loud. Then, amidst the laughter, Janice said, "We've run out of funds in our social service program."

The laughter died down quickly.

"I'm sorry, but we have no money to help you with."

"But... but... we only need $15," explained the woman. "We have been able to get the rest together...." Her voice trailed off.

There was only silence as the three stood there looking for words to say.

"I'm sorry. If you had called first, I could have saved you a trip down," explained Janice.

"We don't have a phone."

After a few moments of silence, Janice simply said, "I'm sorry."

"Thank you," came the muffled response. They walked out slowly, $15 shy of the unreachable goal.

●

And the multitudes asked [John], "What shall we do?" And he answered them, "He who has two coats, let him share with those who have none; and him who has food, likewise...."
[Luke 3:10–11]

Blessed are you poor, for yours is the Kingdom of Heaven.
[Luke 6:20]

●

Hear me, O Lord, as I strive to share the blessings that you have
  bestowed upon me with all your children. Hear me admit
  that I know that I proclaim a better Gospel than I live.
I am too often cowed by the majority who tell me that the poor
  deserve their fate, the homeless choose a life with no shelter,
  and there are people who do not want to work.
Sometimes I am ashamed of the beginnings that you called me to:
         the towel,
                the sharing,
                       the love,
                             the cross...
Give me, O Lord,
the courage that comes from knowing that Christ Jesus means to
  win that for which he dies: the lives of all his brothers and
  sisters;
the commitment to service that is born and nourished when we
  follow your example of service;
the quality of life that comes when the cost of discipleship is
  declared and your children rise up and answer "Yes, I will!"
Revive my sense of service, O God.
Revive my commitment to share more than token amounts.
Revive the light of my witness to those living in the dark.
Revive the sense of joy that I had when I first followed you.
Revive me, Lord, revive me again.
Through the God of the poor and of all the needy ones.

                                                        Amen.

20

Life Without Hope

Thersa has just left the church. She is a beautiful fifteen-year-old girl who has been attending church since she was ten. She simply showed up one day and asked if she could be a part. Members of the church suspected child abuse at once. Her Sunday School teacher visited her home and found that things were not well. Her mother drank. Her father was away from home most of the time. Thersa's two smaller brothers crawled across the cold, dirty floor. The small public housing apartment was overcrowded with five people and too many roaches to count. On that day, Thersa sat in a corner bruised and aching.

Concerned church members had called the child abuse hot-line. They were asked to call the next time that Thersa was alone at the church so that she might be interviewed by a case worker. A few days later Thersa came to the youth club and the social workers were called.

They asked Thersa a great many questions. "If you could change anything about your home, what would it be?" The frail, stringy-haired blonde pulled her baseball cap down over her eyes. Once in Sunday School she claimed that when her daddy got a job they were going to move to the country. On this day, however, she said nothing about that.

"Would you like for your brothers to be sisters?"

A few days earlier, in the alley beside the church, Thersa had been beaten up by a group of youth for defending her younger brother. The gang called the boys "sissies." Thersa took up for them and it cost her more bruises. Perfectly still, never taking her eyes from the floor, she did not relate the incident. Her bare feet stuck out of her blue jeans that were too short for her already long legs. The bottoms of her feet were black.

"Would you rather your brothers be rabbits?" asked the social worker, obviously irritated that Thersa had nothing to say.

Once Thersa found a kitten. She brought the tiny, hungry creature to the church claiming that her family hates cats. They had owned a dog once but it had been run over; when Thersa would not quit crying, she was whipped and told that those things happened. She cared for the kitten every day at the church until it disappeared. Thersa mentioned none of this. She simply stared down. Her hands were clutched tightly together. Her eyes never left the floor. Quietly, coldly, she said nothing.

The social worker shrugged her shoulders and left, whispering that the church should call if the child should decide to talk.

Shortly afterwards, Thersa left. She never said anything. She appeared not to feel anything. She did not return to the church for a long time.

●

Vanity! Vanity! Utter meaningless! All is vanity.
[Ecclesiastes 1:2]

●

Lord,
some days I feel nothing.
The motivation to keep at it is gone.
I am tired of trying to make things a little better in a world that
    is never any better.
I am weary of watching my concerned action go for naught.
I need more returns on my investments of love.
I am spent.
I feel that there is nothing more that I can give.
I feel nothing.
O God, to feel nothing is to die.
To cease living.
No more pain.
No more joy.
No more hunger.
No more conviction.
No more love.
No more life.
Nothing.
O God, may I always feel.
May I never stop.
Something...
Anything...
At fifteen, one so young felt nothing.
O Lord, at fifteen she was dead.
Resurrect all of us from the powers of nothing.

                                  Amen.

21

The Visit

It was unbelievably hot! The temperature was well over one hundred degrees. Heat in the city seems much more intense than in the country. It bounces off the pavement and is absorbed by the asphalt. The result is stifling. Everyone's energy is drained; tempers run as high as the temperature. Even the children, normally with unlimited, boundless energy, find that it is uncomfortable to play. Everyone seeks shade or air conditioning. Churches often open their buildings as "cool centers" for those who do not have an air conditioner.

We had not seen Mr. Hooper during the heat wave. "Hoopy" is a senior citizen who tended bar for years. When it came time to retire, he had only a social security check to depend on. As is the case for many people in that situation, it was simply not enough. There was a rumor that he lived with a woman who was also on social security. By combining their incomes, they would be able to eke out a meager existence.

Hoopy did not have air conditioning and had been in bad health for the past few months. He had received a pacemaker to control his erratic heartbeat. He had been very nervous about it because he thought that he was too old to have surgery. Since coming home from the hospital, he had not attended church. On this day when it was so very hot, people at the church thought that someone should check on Hoopy, so I went to visit him.

His house on East Liberty Street was a typical shot-gun building. Hoopy's bed was set up in the living room. Pink paint was peeling off the high walls. All that was left of the overhead light fixture were two wires that hung down above the bed. Mouse traps were situated in all four corners of the room. There was no cheese in the set traps. The large television sat next to the bed playing very loudly. There was just enough room for me to stand between the television and the bed.

Hoopy, a short, round man who wore spectacles, lay naked on the bed with a wet towel covering him. Both of us were embarrassed. He talked about the pacemaker; I talked about the church. The television overwhelmed our words. Mostly we sat and tried not to look at each other. I tried to assure him that he would be well and back at the church in no time. I said a quick prayer with him and turned to leave.

As I turned the door knob, I heard a sniffle. Turning back towards the naked man, the loud television, and the peeling paint, I saw that Hoopy was crying. I asked him if everything was all right. He nodded his head up and down as tears continued to roll down his stubbled cheeks. Sitting up on the bed, he embraced me.

"Th-th-th-thanks," he stuttered.

"Sure," I replied.

"Y-you t-t-th-the first to come...," his voice trailed off on the last word as he cried.

I hugged him for a long time. Later, when I went outside, I was the one crying.

●

Those who are well have no need of a Physician, but those who are sick do. I have not come to call the righteous, but sinners to repentance.

[Luke 5:32]

●

Lord,
there are hurting sisters and brothers who are all around me.
Most of the time I am much too busy to notice them.
It is only in extreme circumstances that I think of them.
It is only during tragedies that I am concerned.
Most of the time I pay scant attention to them.
I am unaware of their needs.
I am uncertain of their status.
I am ignorant of their relationship with you.
You came to establish a people of compassion.
The example of your life was one of loving concern for those in
    need around you.
When you encountered need, Lord Jesus, you met it.
Too often, when I encounter need, I ignore it.
Or put it off.
Lord, there are people who need me now.
There are people who need you now.
Free me of my selfish agenda, Lord,
so that I will be free to serve you through others.

                                                    Amen.

22

The River Rat

Many people at the mission and on the street considered Florence Bryson to be a river rat. A woman of seventy-five, she had jet black hair. Her face was scarred with the weight of her years. She looked like a bag lady, although she had her own place. She always wore two or three coats on top of her sweater. Even in the heat of summer, it was not uncommon to see her pacing the streets of the neighborhood with a red beanie-cap pulled down low over her head. Sweat would pour down the little bit of face that showed. Her smell testified that she always needed a bath.

Her talent was to take empty packs of cigarettes and fashion them into picture frames. As she walked the sidewalks of the community she would stop whenever she saw a discarded cigarette wrapper, pick it up, and very carefully straighten it out. After she collected enough, she would begin folding them so that they interlocked. Weaving the colors of the various brands together, the frame would have a flavor all its own. The countless pictures of her son, Elvis, of the singer by the same name, and of Jesus displayed in her small home were all within such frames. She was proud of her talent.

She was not liked very well in the neighborhood. The kids would call her names and throw things at her. Once, someone threw a rock at her, striking her in the head and knocking her to the dirty pavement. A stranger rushed to offer assistance. When he approached, Florence began to scream and curse. She scurried away from the would-be savior.

Whenever she came to the church, it was always for assistance.

In a little-girl-voice that was in sharp contrast to her appearance, the River Rat would ask, "Do you think that you might be able to help me with a few canned goods?" The church always helped. She would always promise to come to a worship service, but she never did.

Florence died during one of the hottest summers ever. It was on a Saturday or Sunday. No one is sure which. It was well over one hundred degrees. Her body was lying across the bed. She had on the cap and a couple of coats. Her arms were both cocked in the air so that it appeared she was imitating a mummy. Her feet were on the floor. It looked as if she had sat down on the bed and had fallen backwards as people do when they are tired. A fan was blowing so that the hot air circulated around the room. She would not have to worry about the kids throwing things at her any longer.

She was buried in an unmarked grave at Potter's Field a few days later. There was no funeral. Few even noticed that she was gone. Her mouth was too foul for most. The lonesome way in which she carried herself kept most people at bay. She was forever asking and never giving. But I liked her. Sometimes, when I am walking the streets, I still look for her.

●

If you do not oppress the alien, the sojourner, or the widow,
...then I will let you live in this place.

[Jeremiah 7:6]

●

Lord of the lost and the forgotten,
There are so many of your children — my sisters and
   brothers — that I do not remember.
Hurt ones,
   wounded ones,
      lonely ones,
         sick ones,
            dying ones,
               dead ones.
We are like sheep without a shepherd.
Heal the sheep who are wounded.
Touch those who are in pain.
Clean the sheep who are soiled.
Warm the ones who are cold.
Comfort the sheep who are frightened.
Find the sheep who are lost.
Bring them together.
Show all of us that a land built on justice is the pathway to a
   new land.
A promised land.
The Kingdom.
Renew us all so that we might renew one another.
In the name of the Good Shepherd,
Jesus the Christ.

Amen.

23

The Truth Shall Set You Free

"True! True!," came the cries from around the table. Micki, a young student from the seminary, lowered her head and smiled. She was enjoying the moment of triumph. "No, it's false!" she exclaimed. "I haven't even been to New York!"

"But you described it in such detail," said Cindy, the associate pastor of the church.

After our common meal at the end of the day we had time for interaction. Sometimes the people at the table would pray. On occasion, we would simply sit and talk. And sometimes we played games. On this night we played "True or False." Everyone tells a story about themselves that may be either true or false. Those listening have to decide which. It is an enjoyable way for very diverse people to grow to know one another a little more intimately.

And it was a very diverse group of individuals that had gathered. Young and vivacious, Cindy naturally becomes a part of any conversation. Her husband, Robert, is quiet and subdued beside her. Every Monday evening they participate in the meal. Chester, former street alcoholic and current church cook, prepared the common meal every night for anyone who wished to come. By 5:30 when the meal was served, however, he was much too full from snacking to eat with everyone else. Sonny also sat at the table. A skinny, short man of fifty, Sonny once lived on the streets, but after joining the church, he became the errand man for the church. If someone needs something, Sonny might complain a great deal, but he will always deliver.

"It's Robert's turn," someone said.

Straight-faced, Robert said, "Once I spent three months back-packing across Alaska with a shaved head."

"False! False!" came the cries from around the table.

Long-haired Robert smiled. "It's true," he said with a smile.

"Your turn," they said to Ray. Ray is a one of the three mentally ill residents that lives at the church. A schizophrenic, Ray stands off to one side of the table. He will only take bread and water. He often sleeps in the hallway. Still, Ray is a great help around the church. Everyone likes him.

"Well," he began, "once my mother sent me out to shovel the snow from our sidewalk. The snow was really deep and I had a real hard time making any headway. Then I noticed that blood was coming out of the snow. I looked down and saw that there were bodies. That is where the blood was coming from." He stopped his monotone discourse to draw a breath. "Every time I stuck my shovel into the snow I would hit a body. They were everywhere. It was horrible!"

Everyone around the table was silent for a moment. Every eye was on Ray. "False," said Cindy. "False! False!" echoed the others from around the table. Everyone grew quiet and waited for Ray's response.

With a sly smile on his face he quietly said, "Could be, but I sure believed it at the time."

●

Jesus then said to the Jews who had believed in him, "If you continue in my word, then you are truly my disciples, and you will know the truth and the truth shall make you free."

[John 8:32–33]

●

Lord Jesus,
it is difficult to discern your truth these days.
I am hard pressed to find any real truth.
Things are not black and white as some would have me believe.
There are not just good people and bad.
There are no easy answers.
To complicate things, O God, there are so many proclaiming that
　　they are speaking for you. Sometimes, people I know will
　　follow one of these "spokespeople" for a while, but they often
　　end up disappointed or disillusioned.
Lord, I long for the freedom that you claim comes from knowing
　　the truth of the word. I used to think that you meant the
　　written word. Now I know that it is that and more. I keep
　　bumping into you in the greyness of life that is somewhere
　　between absolute truth and absolute falseness.

Amen.

The Prophetess

Madelyn is a prophetess. She doesn't look much like folks would expect one to look like. She lives in a nice house in the suburbs. She has raised children who are model students at school and active participants in her church. She is married to a man who has a comfortable job. She is a Sunday School teacher in the large suburban church that she attends. She wears nice clothes and drives a new automobile. In her forties, she has hair that is just beginning to gray. She looks like thousands of other white, middle-class, conservative women in America. Nevertheless, Madelyn is a prophetess.

After volunteering to develop a Girl Scout troop in the inner city, Madelyn has come to love and understand many of the problems of "her girls" and their families. Not long after beginning, Madelyn had the girls wearing uniforms, carrying flags, holding special services, and doing community service. The mothers of the troop members noticed a change in their daughters and came to see. A few weeks later, some of the mothers became regular volunteers with the Girl Scout troop or some other activity of the church.

At one meeting, some of the girls told Madelyn of the death of an infant in the housing project. During the night, the child had died of crib death. Madelyn immediately called for the troop to pray for the family. After the meeting was over, Madelyn visited the mother in the housing project. She tried to comfort those who would not be comforted. Mostly, she just sat.

Those who were grieving with the mother noticed a commotion

outside the thickly screened window. Madelyn peered out and saw that a television crew from a local station was setting up, and she walked out to see why. The reporter told her that he had come to do the story on "the woman who had beaten her baby and later discovered it dead in a crib full of roaches." In horror, Madelyn said that it was a vicious rumor with no truth behind it. The reporter smiled and went on planning for the live six o'clock telecast. Madelyn turned and began to walk away.

A crowd of interested onlookers formed around the reporter. Madelyn paused and surveyed the scene: the confused eyes of the children she worked with; the run-down housing project they lived in; the filth and the garbage in the street; the unemployed men who passed their days playing an endless game of basketball.

And she saw the clean, white, blow-dried smile of the reporter. She saw injustice, and seeing transformed her.

With a determined look, Madelyn turned and marched back to the reporter. "Excuse me," she began, "but this is wrong! You have come here to exploit the grief of a woman — almost a baby herself — who has just lost her baby! The baby died of crib death. It happens sometimes. There was no abuse. There were no roaches in the crib, although they are everywhere else. And you come in here to make news! If this had happened in the suburbs, you would have left the family alone to grieve in peace, but because it happens here you decide it is news. Well, it's wrong! Do you hear me? It's just not right!" She turned and marched back to the church.

The reporter stood for a few moments considering her words. He looked around and saw the crowd, the garbage in the streets, the never ending game of basketball, and the dirty apartments.

Then he lifted the microphone, pointed to the camera, and began the broadcast. "A baby was horribly beaten to death downtown today," he began. "Details in a few minutes."

•

He judged the cause of the poor and the needy; then it was well. Is not this to know me? says the Lord.

[Jeremiah 22:16]

•

Lord of the just and the unjust,
we live in a divided world:
of rich and poor,
of black, red, yellow, and white,
of educated and illiterate,
of our kind of people and "that" kind of people.
There are the just and the unjust.
People do not understand each other.
People do not take time to understand each other.
As a result, hate grows, terrorism kills, there are wars and rumors
of wars.
Help me risk understanding others, Lord.
And help me to speak the truth as a result.

Amen.

"I had heard about Jesus for a long time.
I heard he was in the Bible or in some church or another.
Sometimes I would go looking for him in the those places,
but I never found him.
Then one day I stumbled across him.
He was in the faces of people at the church.
I knew right then that I wanted to be a part."

THE RESURRECTION IS NOW!
Matthew 28:1–10

> Never did Paul or Peter or Stephen point to an empty tomb
> as evidence of the resurrection. The evidence was the spirit-
> filled fellowship.
>
> — *Clarence Jordan*

They went to look for his body. They went at great risk, for
the political climate was still very tense. These women had been
involved with Jesus and his small band. Going to the tomb to
embalm the corpse was much like going to lay flowers on the grave
of a guerrilla fighter. He had been an outlaw. He had attacked
the status quo and the establishment. He had organized a mob of
poor, sick, left-out, and lonely people and marched into the Temple
to take it over from the leaders.

He had been publicly executed so that everyone would know
that fancy big-time Temples and political leaders have no use for
the ideas that Jesus advocated and that anyone who had any
thought about picking up where Jesus had left off could expect
the same punishment. His disciples were too scared to show their
faces in public, but these women had great love for their dead Savior, and great love can overcome any fear. So they went to the
tomb.

They found an empty tomb. They went to embalm a corpse,
but there wasn't any corpse. They might have expected as much.
Very often, the bodies of freedom fighters are done away with so
that no monument can be established to inspire the people. So
they cried; their worst fears had come true. His body had been
stolen. It was probably at the bottom of the Sea of Galilee by now.

But as they left the empty tomb, they were "met by Jesus, and he said, 'Hail!' And they came and took hold of his feet and they worshipped him. And then Jesus said, 'Do not be afraid; go and tell my brothers and sisters to go to Galilee, and there they will see me.'"

Why Galilee? There Jesus had laid down the principles of the Kingdom of God. He had stated what his ministry was about: liberty to the captives and freedom for the oppressed. The Sermon on the Mount had been taught there and the hungry had been fed. The dirty fishermen and the despised prostitutes had been brought into one family. Jesus told his "brothers and sisters" to go back and start doing these things and you will "see me."

The reason that so many of us never see the resurrected Jesus is that we don't do what Jesus told us to do. Instead, we relegate Jesus, and his message, to heaven. We confine him to another time and another place so we will not have to deal with the things that he says that his "brothers and sisters" must deal with. As the brothers and sisters do the deeds of the Kingdom, God will give us the gift of the Kingdom. And we will see the resurrected Jesus. A new family will be born, and a new society will be established. And a living Jesus will reign.

The resurrection is not just "back then." The resurrection is now! It was not just for Jesus; it is for all who wish to be a part of the family of God. It is not just a resurrection of a corpse; it is the uplifting of a dead life to a new one. It is not a prolongation of life; it is a new life here and now. We do not have to wait until we get to heaven, for the resurrection is now. We do not have to wait for life after death, for the resurrection is now! And that makes all the difference. A dead church can be made alive again, and a dead faith can be made alive again.

You who have lost faith and no longer have anything to believe in, who now have only despair and doubt and emptiness, the resurrection is now! Come and believe again.

You who have been hurt in a relationship, who have been abused and broken, you who have had your trust broken down and the defenses of hostility have turned you inward, the resurrection is now! Come and love again.

You who have lost faith in an institutional church that seems to care more about buildings than people and more about numbers than individuals, the resurrection is now! Come and be a part of a spirit-filled fellowship.

You who have lost the ability to stand on your own two feet and now need the crutches of alcohol or drugs or images of yourself that are falsely induced, the resurrection is now! Come and lean on Jesus and on his brothers and sisters.

You who are tired of playing games with yourselves and with other people, who pretend to be someone you are not and who convince other people that you are something you are not, the resurrection is now! Come and be loved as you are.

You who are depressed over the nuclear cloud that hangs over our heads and leaders who are warmakers and care nothing for peace, the resurrection is now! Come under the prince of peace and join a family of peacemakers.

You who have known only sickness and too much death, the resurrection is now! Come and be a part of a new life.

You who have known hunger and poverty or who are tired of fighting losing battles against the causes of hunger and poverty, the resurrection is now! Come and eat of the Bread of Life and be filled, and learn how we can overcome poverty and hunger.

You who lack assurance in life and in God, the resurrection is now! Come and find blessed assurance and see the resurrected Jesus.

You who are disappointed about where your life has left you, who have been laid off or left behind or left out, the resurrection is now! Come and be included as a worker for a new Kingdom.

You who are tired of the inconsistency of life, who are tired of the ups and downs, who are tired of going too far or not far enough, the resurrection is now! Come and know the security of a resurrected life with Jesus and his brothers and sisters.

You who are tired of a dead-end lifestyle, the resurrection is now! Come and find a new life of love and peace and familyhood.

Know that the resurrection is now! Jesus was resurrected first. Now it is our turn. Come and join the Society of Salty Saints. Be resurrected now!